College Football's Great Dynasties
MICHIGAN

College Football's Great Dynasties

MICHIGAN

Melissa Larson

SMITHMARK

Published by Smithmark Publishers
112 Madison Avenue
New York, New York 10016

Produced by
Brompton Books Corp.
15 Sherwood Place
Greenwich, CT 06830

ISBN 0-8317-3476-0

Printed in Hong Kong

10 9 8 7 6 5 4 3 2 1

Page 1: *Eric Kattus celebrates his touchdown in the Maryland game in September, 1985.*

Page 2: *Michigan quarterback Jim Harbaugh lets a pass fly in the Ohio State game of 1986.*

Page 3: *The Michigan team jogs off the field at halftime during the 1986 Ohio State game.*

Below: *"Glory in the Mud": A Michigan halfback gains 25 yards against Penn in November, 1937. Michigan won the game, played in Philadelphia, by a score of 7-0.*

PICTURE CREDITS

All photographs courtesy of UPI/Bettmann
Newsphotos except the following:
Joseph Arcure: 65(bottom).
Chance Brockway: 2, 3, 7, 58, 59, 60, 62, 64,
    66(bottom), 67(center left, center right), 68,
    69(both), 70, 71(top), 72, 73(top), 74(all three),
    75(all four), 76(both), 77(top).
Malcolm Emmons: 6, 63, 66(top right), 67(bottom),
    77(bottom).
Dale Fisher: 61(bottom).
Robert Kalmbach: 65(top).
Per H. Kjeldsen: 67(top right), 71(bottom).
Ohio State University Photo Archives: 53(top).
University of Michigan Athletic Department:
    15(bottom), 23, 24(top), 25(bottom), 27(top right),
    37(bottom), 43(bottom), 44(top), 47, 55(bottom),
    56, 61(top), 66(top left, center left), 67(top left).
University of Michigan Athletic Department
    Collection, Bentley Historical Library,
    University of Michigan: 8(top), 10-11(all five), 12-
    13(both), 14, 15(top), 16, 17(both), 19(both), 20(all
    three), 21, 22(both), 24(bottom), 25(top), 26,
    27(center, bottom left, bottom right), 28, 29(top
    right), 30, 31, 32, 33(bottom), 34, 35, 37(top), 38,
    40-41, 40(bottom), 43(top), 44(bottom), 45(top
    left), 49.

ACKNOWLEDGMENTS

The author and publisher would like to thank the
following people who have helped in the
preparation of this book: Sydney L. Mayer and
Barbara Thrasher, who edited it; Don Longabucco,
who designed it; Rita Longabucco, who did the
picture research; and Florence Norton, who
prepared the index.

Contents

Preface

To many of college football's faithful, the University of Michigan is a treasured constant, a place in the great Midwest where glory still abides when all the other good teams in the land seem to come from the Southeast or West Coast or South Bend, Indiana.

For others, of course, Michigan is a pain in the rear, a perennial irritation like the mosquitoes of summer, an institution claiming as its own the letter "M" and the color blue. How dare they come swaggering into town to wreck your Big-10 Homecoming? Why is it always a Michigan game that pre-empts the one you wanted to watch on a Saturday afternoon – they can't have *that* many fans – can they? And why is it that of all the goofy animal team nicknames, theirs actually seems to fit them? You try to tell yourself that the Wolverine

Right: *Michigan quarterback Rick Leach confers with Bo Schembechler and an assistant coach on the sidelines in 1978. Leach was one of Schembechler's most successful quarterbacks.*

stripes look silly on their helmets – but by then they've rolled up 35 points, and you're forced to spend the rest of the afternoon pondering the unfairness of it all . . . .

Yet the University of Michigan has had its share of disappointments, failures and long, dreary, winless spells. In between Yost's thrilling Point-A-Minute success and the exploits of Crisler's bonecrushers led by Tom Harmon, there were wilted hopes, disappointed alumni and ruined autumn days. There were Wolverine teams playing their hearts out in anonymity. Before Bo came along, Michigan fans spent the entire decade of the fifties and the early half of the sixties watching hated Ohio State grab most of the glory. There are those who say that a Michigan quarterback will never achieve success in the NFL. And, of course, the ghosts of loused-up Rose Bowls haunt the dreams of modern fans.

But the spirit of Michigan football helps fans weather the lows, and rejoice in the good times with a hearty sort of zest. As an Iowa student during the Hawkeyes' bleak period of the mid-1970s, I found I couldn't even hate Michigan for beating us year after year. There was something about the conduct of the players and coaches that commanded my unwilling respect. They never ran up the score. There was no strut-

ting cockiness, no belief in their own invincibility or in some divine intervention. They did what they had to do, took the win gratefully and went home to Ann Arbor.

I'd like to believe that the spirit of Michigan is a reflection of good Midwestern values: closeness to nature, heartland work ethic. In reality, it is probably the fact that the Wolverines have been coached and led, decade after decade, by men with wisdom as well as great skill – men with an honest fear of failure and an understanding of their own weaknesses. From Fielding Yost to Bo Schembechler, and into the future with Gary Moeller, Michigan coaches have keenly felt a responsibility to mold the young men in their charge. They've taught the Wolverines to take nothing for granted – and most, even in this cynical age, have learned that lesson.

However, the winning tradition affects each graduate, whether they know it or not. There's a simple confidence about Wolverines that can drive other people crazy. My friend Lynn, a Michigan graduate, was recently my guest at her first Chicago Bears home game at Soldier Field. As we entered the stands, I expected her to gasp in awe. Instead, she almost chuckled and said, "What a cute little stadium!"

Go Blue, I inwardly sighed.

Above: *An offensive formation in practice in 1902: Fielding Yost's famous Point-A-Minute teams dominated the early years of this century.*

Right: *Michigan's only Heisman Trophy winner, Tom Harmon, gains five yards in a 19-13 triumph over Penn at Michigan Stadium in 1938.*

Opposite: *Michigan players, along with fans, celebrate Coach Schembechler's first and most famous triumph over Ohio State, 24-12, in his first year as Michigan head coach in 1969. Schembechler is not visible.*

1. The Early Years 1880-1899

The first intercollegiate football game west of the Alleghenies took place between the University of Michigan and Racine College on May 30, 1879. The baseball grounds at Chicago's White Stocking Park were chosen as the site of the contest. It was a day long remembered by Michigan athletes and supporters.

Football had only recently begun to disentangle itself from its rugby roots. "Scrummages" gave either team access to the ball, and kept the action moving in an exhausting manner up and down the field. An emphasis on defense meant there was hardly ever any scoring in those early days.

Nevertheless, midway through the first "inning" Michigan found itself scrambling toward the Racine goal. Just then a young civil engineering student named Irving "Ike" Pond – lithe and gymnastic – engraved himself in Michigan lore forever with a headlong rush that recorded the first touchdown. No points were awarded – the outcome depended on which team scored more of them, and a kicked field goal counted for four touchdowns! Yet Pond had drawn first blood, and the assembled fans cheered heartily. They rejoiced in Ann Arbor as well, for the students and fans back home were receiving regular telegraph reports posted on a board near the medical building.

Later, Ike Pond described the game week, and hinted at the glory involved in being a football player, even in those days: "On Wednesday evening the eleven appeared on campus for the first time in their new suits. They presented quite a neat appearance. The uniform is of white canvas, close fitting, with blue stockings and belt. A large number of spectators came out to see the boys practice. They were opposed by a picked eleven. The team left Thursday on the day express. A few of the students, among them our managing editor, accompanied them as spectators."

Pond went on to an architectural career, designing several Michigan campus buildings. Yet he remained most famous for his exploits on that one autumn afternoon. His

Right: *Program for the Penn-Michigan game in 1911.*

Far right: *Stylized Michigan program for the Cornell game in 1917.*

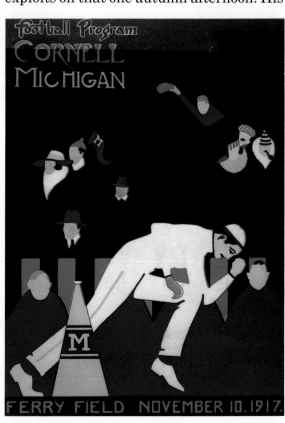

Far left: *Program for the Minnesota-Michigan game of 1923, for the "Little Brown Jug."*

Left: *Program for the game dedicating the opening of Michigan Stadium in 1927. The facility, since expanded, is still the world's largest college football stadium. Originally built to hold 72,000, it has since grown to accommodate well over 100,000. Michigan won the game, 21-0.*

Left: *Midwest meets East: Program for the Harvard game in 1929.*

excellent rushing and headlong dives had earned him the crowd's cheers of "Pond Forever." Michigan later tallied a field goal to clinch the victory over Racine and begin its long love affair with the game of American football.

Michigan football had experienced a shaky beginning preceding that historic contest. Born in 1869 at schools like Harvard, Yale and Princeton – Eastern universities with British public school traditions – football was a constantly-evolving combination of rugby rules, a newly-designed oblong pig's bladder for a ball, and plenty of Yankee mayhem. There were no consistent rules, and many eastern administrators dismissed the new game out of hand as bestial – some prohibited football on their campuses entirely. What they didn't understand was that the game was springing up all over the country by 1880. It was too late to put the genie back in the bottle.

Football games between Michigan lower- and upperclassmen had been played under the so-called English rules since soon after the game's first official 1869 contest between Princeton and Rutgers. Basically, the English rules dictated the game be played like rugby as far as offense, defense and putting the ball into play were concerned, but with 11 players on a side. Teams from different geographical areas, however, tended to be accustomed to different sets of guidelines, and often spent months or years negotiating by mail the rules governing upcoming contests before a date

and site could actually be agreed upon.

Michigan footballers thought they had struck a deal in 1873 with like-minded Cornell for a game to be played at the neutral midpoint of Cleveland, Ohio. The date was set and all that remained was to obtain the blessing of school administrators. Cornell president Andrew White, however, was to prove one of the game's first party-poopers with his high-handed letter to Michigan president James Angell. "No, I will not per-

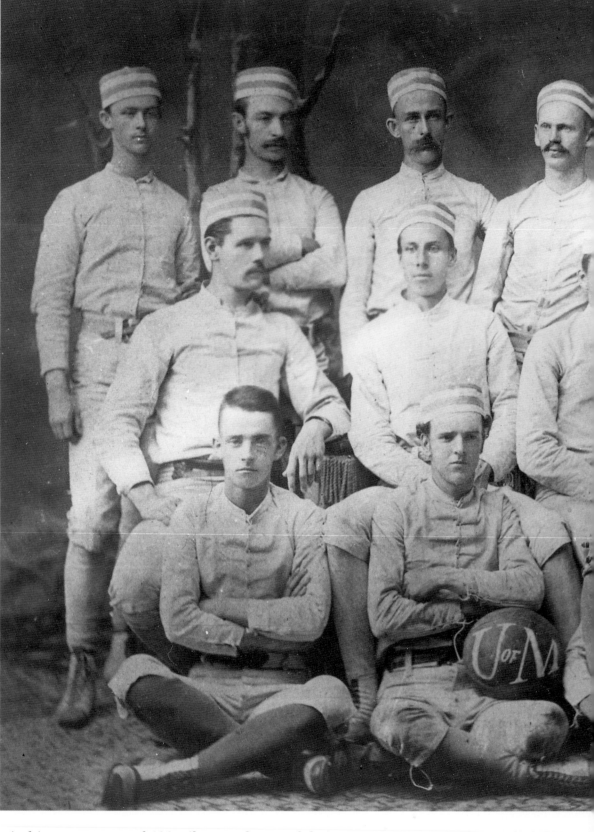

Right: *Michigan's first football team in 1879. The team came out of the season with a paltry 1-0-1 record. Uniforms bore little resemblance to those in use today.*

mit thirty men to travel 400 miles merely to agitate a bag of wind," was his stern refusal. Cornell players would wait another 14 years for the chance to try their skills against another school.

By 1879, the year of the Racine victory, Michigan football and baseball players had formed an alliance called the Athletic Association, and were raising money among students and alumni to build a gymnasium of their own.

Games with the University of Toronto followed in the next two years, as football sprouted and grew in Ann Arbor. Banquets and brass bands, and groups of cheering students at the train station began to greet each new Michigan football contest. After achieving a scoreless tie and a win against Toronto, Michigan footballers boldly scheduled meetings with Harvard, Yale and

week on November 4 by falling to Princeton, one goal and two touchdowns to none. By all accounts, they had done admirably against the best in the nation, and Michigan was soon after accorded the honor of being invited to join the Eastern College League. It is not to be underestimated that the giants of the new game recognized in this Midwestern band of stalwarts the potential for stiff competition. Very likely none of the Eastern players had ever been west of Philadelphia before.

While they declined the invitation, Michigan scheduled games with Yale and Harvard again in 1883. By this time, shifting sets of rules began to factor as much in football contests as did the skill of the participants. When Michigan players arrived for their contest against Yale, they were informed that the new oblong ball and a new scoring system would be used. A safety would count one point, a touchdown two points, a goal after a touchdown four, and a goal from the field, five.

All it meant to Michigan was that they lost to Yale 46-0 instead of by a somewhat lower tally. But by continuing to test itself against Yale and Harvard, Michigan was learning new strategies and bettering itself by leaps and bounds. After all, Yale's player-coach was Walter Camp, the "Father of Football" who had single-handedly fashioned most of the rules which forever separated American football from rugby. Camp instituted the line of scrimmage from which play would start, and first thought of marking the "gridiron" lines on the field so that yardage could be more accurately measured.

Below: *Michigan's 1884 football team poses before a romantic prop. The team, which went unbeaten and unscored upon, kicked off the University of Michigan's 1884-1887 unbeaten streak.*

Princeton for one unforgettable week in 1881.

Thus, the champions of the Midwest, at least in their own minds, boarded the train to travel to the Eastern schools where, they knew, the best football was being played.

In one bruising week Michigan lost to Harvard by only one touchdown to none, scared the daylights out of Yale before bowing by two goals, then capped the autumn

From 1883 to 1890, however, Michigan concentrated on Midwestern rivals, of which there were now several. There they dominated, winning eight straight games from 1884 to 1887 and holding every team scoreless, including Notre Dame.

The two rivals met for the first time in 1887 in South Bend as Michigan unveiled a sensational drop kicker named James E. Duffy. They defeated the Irish 8-0, and followed it up with two decisive wins at South Bend the following season, 26-6 and 10-4.

The 1890s saw Michigan football continuing to evolve and developing a style all its own. The University of Michigan was the nation's largest campus, with a head count of 2,153 students in 1889. The school's official colors – maize and blue – had been chosen by the graduating class of 1867. As early as 1861, the students had begun calling themselves Wolverines. Michigan had one of the first hired non-student coaches in Frank Crawford, who was a former Yalie and schooled in Eastern football. He shared duties with Mike Murphy, a former trainer at the Detroit Athletic Club.

By 1892 Michigan was playing an ambi-tious schedule which included Wisconsin and Minnesota (wins), plus Chicago and Northwestern (losses). An unusual game had been played with Purdue. After many of the regular Michigan players inexplicably missed the game, others were injured and all available substitutes were used, the Wolverines were forced to forfeit the game to Purdue, 24-0.

One of those injured was to be Michigan's first black letterman, George Jewett. The former football co-captain and track captain at Ann Arbor High, Jewett performed as a stalwart halfback for two seasons with the Michigan team, then transferred to Northwestern and played there for another two seasons.

After his injury in the Purdue contest, Jewett bounced back five days later to play against Northwestern in Chicago. His character was described by author John Behee in his book *Hail to the Victors*: "As he was tackled, several Northwestern men piled on, leaving Jewett when it was all over with a badly bruised face. 'The crowd was indignant,' reported the student newspaper *The Michigan Daily*, 'and requested

Below: Michigan's 1891 football team included Michigan's first black player, George Jewett. Coached by Mike Murphy and Frank Crawford, the team finished the season 4-5.

Jewett to name the man who had mal-treated him, but this he refused to do . . . .' After sitting out for several minutes, the battered sophomore returned to the game and was heartily cheered."

By 1893 Michigan football had come under the jurisdiction of the faculty, for several good reasons. The program was constantly on the brink of financial insolvency, and several times faculty and players had made loans to the team so that road trips could take place as scheduled. More important, however, was the fact that Michigan, like virtually every other advanced college football team, was having trouble controlling its player roster. Coaches inserted themselves into the lineup when they felt it was warranted, Wolverine players were found not to be enrolled in school at all, and others played six or seven years. Most disturbing of all was evidence that a few Michigan players were actually accepting money to play football.

It is said that the great Walter Camp played seven brilliant seasons for Yale before a bad knee forced him to quit — so Michigan was certainly not alone in bending the somewhat vague rules. However, President James Angell and the Michigan Board of Regents felt that the school's football program must be brought into line with the university as a whole. A Board in Control of Athletics, comprised of five professors and four students, was created. Its purpose was to hire all coaches and trainers, and in general supervise Michigan's athletic programs. The Athletic Association essentially ceased to exist and reportedly turned over $6,095.03 in cash and

Above: *The Cornell game in 1894 was held at the Detroit Athletic Club Field.*

Left: *University of Michigan President James Angell kept close control over the football program for over 30 years. The story goes that he personally signed every check issued throughout his entire tenure as President, which was the longest in Michigan history.*

bonds to the new governing Board.

In creating the Board, the University Senate decreed that the position of Graduate Manager of Athletics be established, and in 1898 Charles A. Baird became Michigan's first Athletic Director – the first in a long and famous line.

In February of 1896 a meeting at Chicago's Palmer House Hotel laid the foundation for the nation's most famous

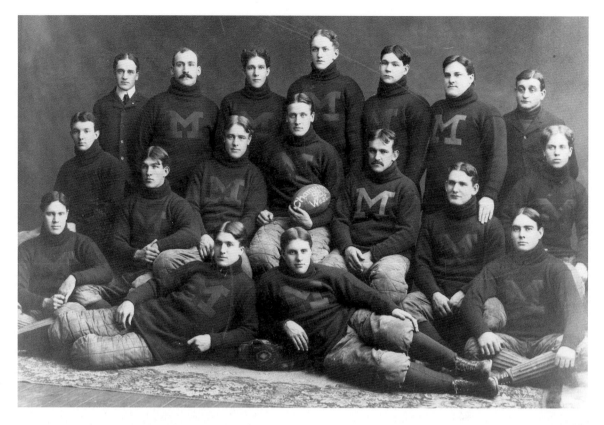

Right: A team photo of the 1898 Champions of the West, who inspired Louis Elbel to write his immortal song, "The Victors." This dominating team allowed only 28 points against their 193, on their way to a 10-0 record.

Opposite top: *A practice scrimmage at Ferry Field, where all Michigan home games were played until 1927.*

Opposite bottom: *A trio of Michigan centers in 1900. In the middle is Tug Wilson, who became Big-10 Commissioner in the 1940s.*

athletic conference. Representatives of seven Midwestern universities met to form an association that would establish common standards and controls of intercollegiate athletics. Michigan, Illinois, Northwestern, Chicago, Purdue, Wisconsin and Minnesota were present. These men demonstrated the foresight to realize that geographical proximity and repeated clashes within the new conference would make for strong rivalries. They were to be proven right year after year.

The University of Michigan would have its differences with the Western Conference, as it was then called, over the years. They were to drop out altogether for nearly a decade. Yet overall the athletic interests of each member school would be admirably advanced by this trailblazing organization. The Western Conference was probably the first to ban payments for players, to establish conference-wide rules for player eligibility, and to firmly enforce central control over these early athletic programs.

Conference leadership was instrumental in advancing the idea that these were, after all, young men, who as athletes were vulnerable to professional gamblers, criminals and other corrupt individuals eager to influence the outcomes of games. America was wild about sports, and the student athletes would be subject to more press, public adulation and scorn than was healthy. That is, unless they were protected from harm by those older and wiser than they. In this task, the conference succeeded admirably for decades.

A game in 1898 against football power

Chicago remains fixed forever in Michigan lore. Michigan had had its troubles competing in the new conference. The University of Chicago, coached by the larger-than-life Amos Alonzo Stagg, was a perennial powerhouse in those early days, along with Wisconsin.

However, the Wolverine team of 1898 was a special one – sweeping through the season with wins over Notre Dame, Northwestern and Illinois on successive Saturdays. Meanwhile, Chicago had only one loss. More important, they had football's best back, Clarence Herschberger. Both teams were undefeated within the conference, so a crowd of 10,000 turned out on Thanksgiving Day in Chicago to see the issue decided.

It was one of those magical moments that are frozen in time. Late in the game, a small Wolverine halfback named Charles Widman ran 65 yards for a touchdown as twilight descended. Michigan won the game, 12-11. In the stands, a young music student named Louis Elbel joined in the victory celebration with the other Michigan students who had traveled south for the game. Elbel struggled to put his elation into words, and the result was a little ditty that has become rather famous:

Hail to the Victors valiant,
Hail to the conquering heroes,
Hail, hail to Michigan
The leaders and best;

Hail to the Victors valiant,
Hail to the conquering heroes,

Hail, hail to Michigan
The Champions of the West.

Years later, Elbel remembered his emotions: "There was never a more enthusiastic Michigan student than I, but that team and that Chicago game pushed me way up in the clouds, and all I had to do was fill in the notes, and there was 'The Victors'."

As Wolverine fans hummed the new song, Michigan celebrated its first conference championship. Its junior center, William Ralph Cunningham, was accorded the honor of being named to Walter Camp's prestigious All-America team. Along with Chicago's Herschberger, he was the first player so named from the Big-10. It was a long-overdue acknowledgment from staunch Easterner Camp that there were talented players out in the Heartland too.

So Michigan football was rolling. Baird was directing athletics full-time – at the princely salary of $2,000 per year. The fledgling Michigan Band of 30 men was now playing the new fight song at every home game. But one more ingredient was needed to bring the whole picture into focus. It arrived in Ann Arbor in 1901 in the small person of Fielding Yost.

2. A New Century 1900-1917

Right: *Father of Wolverine football: Michigan Coach Fielding Yost won more games and had a longer tenure than any coach in Michigan history.*

Michigan legend has it that this conversation took place when Charlie Baird first met his newly-hired football coach, Fielding Yost. As Yost, as always impeccably dressed, walked toward him, Baird introduced himself and remarked that he looked rather young to have had such coaching success with Ohio Wesleyan, Nebraska, Kansas and Stanford.

Fielding Yost replied, "Mr. Baird, there are three things that make a winning football team. Spirit, manpower and coaching. If your boys love Meeshegan, they've got the spirit, you see. If they'll turn out, that takes care of the manpower. I'll take care of the coaching."

Charlie Baird smiled and shook his head as he told Yost, "Well, you've got a real job ahead of you. You've got to beat Chicago."

Thus the supremely confident Yost began the coaching task that would insure his place in Wolverine legend. The 30-year-old had indeed experienced success in coaching: all five of his previous teams had achieved conference championships, and he had coached several of them simultaneously. Yost was, above all, an innovator. He believed that a successful offense needed speed, and this attitude flew in the face of the mania of the day for brute defensive strength above all else.

His early Michigan practices must have been noisy; Yost was forever admonishing his new players to get on with it. Quarterbacks were instructed to call the next play while still on the ground from the previous one. "Are you just a spectator?" he would chasten a laggard lineman between plays. "Hurry up! Hurry up!" Inevitably, a Detroit sportswriter gave him the nickname "Hurry Up" Yost.

Yost was nothing if not opinionated. He even had a few words to say about the new Michigan fight song: "I reckon it's a good thing Louis Elbel was a Meeshegan student when he wrote that song. If he'd been at any other Big-10 school, they wouldn't have had much chance to use it, y'know."

Born and raised in the hill country of West Virginia, Yost had crisscrossed the United States coaching football, obtaining

a law degree, becoming an expert on the rules and forming a lifelong love for the game and for teaching that game to his players. He insisted that they, too, know the rules of their game.

As he shoved a playbook into a player's hand on a train trip, he would say, "In football, as in life, you've got to know the rules and your rights."

In his years at Michigan, or "Meeshegan," as he pronounced it, Fielding Yost would come to symbolize Wolverine athletics. He designed the athletic facilities, including the nation's first field house, and helped raise the money to build them. He brought home the football championships year after year, and in due course became athletic director himself. His home in Ann Arbor became a power center in the town – a place where politicians and poor schoolboys alike were entertained and enlightened. He became an active Republican and gave radio speeches on behalf of candidates he favored. Yet first and foremost he was a football coach.

Yost brought more than brains and inventiveness when he arrived in Ann Arbor that long-ago fall of 1901. He had freshman Willie Heston – a player he had brought along with him from San Jose Normal college in California upon departing for Ann Arbor. Together, they would set the college football world on its ear.

Halfback Heston would become one of the first real college football stars and the unstoppable weapon in Yost's new Wolverine football arsenal. A gentle giant, Heston had made a living as a teamster and stevedore after dropping out of San Jose Normal. At Yost's urging, Heston borrowed a train ticket, bought a new suit and headed for Ann Arbor to play football and attend law school. Yost greeted him enthusiastically and added the freshman to a team that

Above left: *Michigan All-American Willie Heston was Yost's greatest star on his Point-A-Minute teams at the turn of the century.*

Above: *Fullback Neil Snow practicing his kicking at old Ferry Field in 1900.*

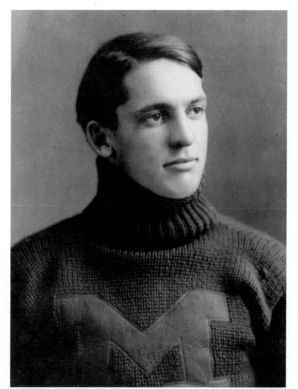

Right: *Captain and quarterback of Michigan's 1901 football team, Harrison "Boss" Weeks.*

Right: *The Minnesota-Michigan game in 1902. Coach Yost wears a hat on the sidelines.*

Below: *Backfield practice for the 1902 Michigan team.*

already boasted brilliant fullback Neil Snow, and quarterback and captain Harrison "Boss" Weeks.

The combination proved devastating. With Heston as a battering ram, the 1901 Wolverines piled up 8,000 yards for 550 points, 11 victories and a perfect season. Along the way someone figured out that Yost's group had scored an average of a point for every minute they played – and the "Point-A-Minute" Michigan nickname was born, a name they would keep for years.

The complete dominance of this team can hardly be overstated. Michigan was beating teams with totals like 107 points over Iowa, 86 points over Ohio State, and 128 points (against 0) over Buffalo. And this was in the days before forward passing, when a touchdown scored just five points! The 5-foot, 8-inch, 184-pound Heston proved to be one of the fastest players in Michigan history – regularly beating Michigan's Olympic sprinting champion, Archie Hahn, in head-to-head 40-yard

MINN. CROSS-BUCK PLAY

COACH YOST

TRAINER FITZPATRICK

Schultz   Hal Weeks   Norcross   Tom Hammond   Longman

dashes. He was also strong enough to drag or carry would-be tacklers into the end zone with him. Wolverine fans soon had a favorite chant: "We Want Heston!"

Nor was the 1901 Western Conference championship the end of that glorious season. The Wolverines were invited to play in Pasadena, California, on New Year's Day of 1902. The idea was to stage a football contest as a sort of grand finale to the city's Tournament of Roses week. After hammering out such details as meal money and expense allotments, Michigan agreed to play Stanford, the Pacific Coast champion.

The Wolverines left Ann Arbor on December 17 with snow on the ground and temperatures below freezing. The train trip west took eight days, during which the Michigan players were accorded every courtesy and received national recognition. However, the ribbing began when the team hit Los Angeles. Michigan would wilt in the heat, said the newspaper reporters.

Besides, they were used to grass fields and the Rose Bowl, as it was by then called, would be played on dirt. Finally, West Coast writers who had seen Willie Heston play at San Jose were none too charitable: if Heston could win a starting job on the Wolverine team, how good could the team be?

They soon found out. After appearing in the Tournament of Roses Parade, outfitted in new uniforms and riding in a large carriage, Michigan proceeded to take Stanford apart in front of some 8000 horrified witnesses. Fake kicks, slashing runs by Heston, and five Neil Snow touchdowns left the score 49-0 with several minutes left in the second half.

Yost must have smiled inwardly as he watched Stanford captain Ralph Fisher approach the Michigan bench. "If you are willing, sir, we are ready to quit," he told Yost. They had several injured players, and no reserves left. One lineman, a cousin of President Theodore Roosevelt, had sus-

Above: *The Michigan football team during the Rose Bowl Parade on New Year's Day, 1902. In this first Rose Bowl, Michigan trounced Stanford 49-0, ending the Rose Bowl game for a time.*

Weeks. Shorts, Snow, Heston, Herrnstein

TACKLE-BACK-RIGHT PLAY.

Top: *Spectators watch the first Rose Bowl game, 1902.*

Above: *Michigan's backfield of Boss Weeks, Neil Snow, Willie Heston and A.E. Herrnstein move forward on an off-tackle play during the Rose Bowl against Stanford on January 1, 1902.*

tained a broken leg and three broken ribs. With Michigan's consent, the first Rose Bowl game was called with eight minutes left on the clock.

Michigan had used only its starting eleven, and Yost later found the four reserves rolling around in the dirt behind the team's hotel in order not to return home with clean uniforms.

An anonymous *Los Angeles Daily Times* reporter summed up the level of competition: "The Michigan backbreakers made monkeys out of the Stanford footballists."

The tournament association, while realizing a profit from the game, pondered the fan interest of similar contests with such lopsided scores – and opted for chariot races the following year. It would be another 16

years before the Rose Bowl football game would be revived. That was their problem. Yost's was putting together another championship team the following season.

The 1902 team lacked All-American and 10-letter winner Neil Snow, but rolled on in the early season, winning its first six games. Looming ahead, however, was Wisconsin. The Wolverines had not played the Badgers in 1901, and the similarly unbeaten Wisconsin group had grumbled at Michigan being chosen conference champ. This 1902 contest, therefore, had a score-settling air about it. It was played in Chicago in front of some 25,000 fans: an unprecedented Midwest crowd. Before a section of the temporary stands at Marshall Field collapsed, delaying the game, Michigan had scored six points on a Heston touchdown run. The Wolverines made it hold up, winning 6-0 and quieting the Wisconsin doubters for the time being.

The following week Michigan rolled up 107 points against Iowa, and newspapers across the country began picking up the Point-A-Minute nickname. Yost's hardy band topped off the season with a victory over Chicago for the second straight year, garnering another championship.

The 1903 season was to throw up a roadblock of sorts. The great leader and quarterback Boss Weeks was gone, but Yost had inserted 139-pound track sprinter Shorty Norcross at quarterback, and for a while the Wolverines rolled on. Seven straight wins early in the season ran the streak to 28, but up ahead were the Golden Gophers of Minnesota.

Minnesota had a leader and innovator of their own in coach Dr. Henry Williams. He had devised a new defense which he hoped would stop Willie Heston, and a crowd of almost 30,000 fans turned up at Minneapolis' Northrop Field to see if it would work.

In one of the most physically punishing games played up to that time, the two undefeated teams staged a nose-to-nose defensive battle that had both teams breathing hard and snarling at the opposition. During an early punt, returners Norcross and Herb Graver were hit immediately and driven down violently by huge Gopher tackles.

Graver staggered to his feet, wiped the blood off a broken nose and turned to Norcross. "Norky," he said, "this is going to be a rough afternoon."

That proved an understatement. A few minutes later Willie Heston was knocked out of the game, along with tackle Joe Maddock. The scoreless war raged up and down the field, with hair flying and bones crunching. With 12 minutes left in the game Maddock, recovered, pierced the Gopher goal line on the third attempt and it appeared the Wolverines were headed for another victory.

However, with the hometown thousands cheering every play, Minnesota started to move down the field. With only two minutes left, a reserve fullback named Egil Boeckmann scored for the Gophers, and fans stormed the field. Some 5,000 fans had to be shooed off the turf so that Gopher captain Ed Rogers could attempt the extra point. The kick was good, and pandemonium reigned. Minnesota had managed to tie the mighty Wolverines, 6-6.

One sportswriter, safe in the press box, wrote, "Everything that wasn't nailed down went high in the air: hats, canes,

Below: *A portrait of the Michigan team of 1901, which scored 550 points against its opponents' 0. Yost is in the middle of the back row.*

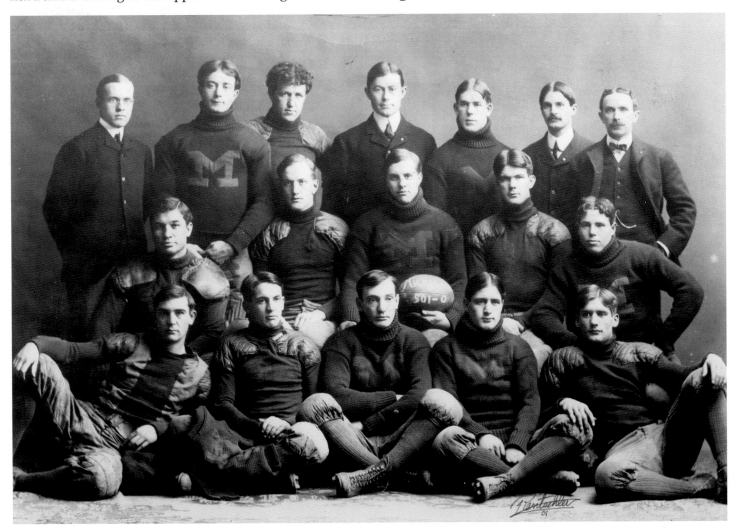

umbrellas and cushions. Dignity was cast to the winds."

The following Monday morning, a janitor found the brown water jug the Michigan team had purchased for use during the game (not trusting even the Minnesota water supply, apparently). Minnesota's athletic director labeled it a "captured Michigan jug." Upon Yost's request that it be returned, the Minnesota Athletic Director replied that if the Wolverines wanted the jug back, they could "come up and win it." Thus was born the Little Brown Jug

Right: *The famous "Little Brown Jug" with the ball from the 1903 game against Minnesota. The jug is still the most famous college football trophy.*

Below: *Michigan halfback Herb Graver breaks through the line during the Indiana game in 1903.*

trophy – which has ever since been the cherished prize belonging to the winner of the Minnesota-Michigan game.

Because of the violence of that 1903 game, it would be six years before Michigan actually "came up" to win the trophy back. The Wolverines won that 1909 contest, and took the jug back with them. Golden Gopher fans didn't see it again for 10 years.

Capping the 1903 season for another Western Conference championship was an easy 28-0 win over Chicago – Yost's third straight over coaching legend A.A. Stagg. And so the Michigan machine steamed on. The 1904 season saw Michigan sweep by 10 straight opponents for a fourth consecutive championship. However, since the Wolverines had played only two conference games they were obliged to share the crown with Minnesota, who had won three conference games. It must have been a bitter pill for Yost to swallow.

Willie Heston left Michigan after the 1904 season, having scored 72 touchdowns in four years, and been selected a consensus All-American in 1903 and 1904. He has remained fixed in Wolverine lore ever since, not only because of his astonishing achievements but because of his loyalty to Yost. "He was like a father to me," Heston would later say of his coach. "He always talked slowly and seriously, and meant what he said. . . . And he was always truthful, and his morals were the best." Yost called Heston the "finest halfback I've ever seen play football." Their relationship had anchored the Point-A-Minute teams.

The 1905 season brought a precipitous end to the Point-A-Minute machine, as a

Left: *Michigan's 1904 team won 10 straight, and a fourth consecutive Western Conference Championship. Germany Schulz is far right.*

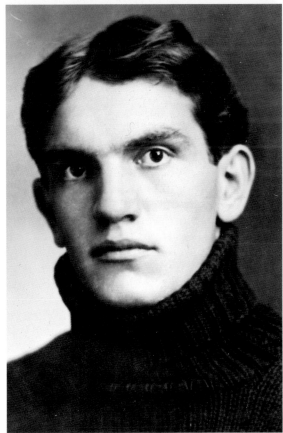

Left: *Adolph "Germany" Schulz was Michigan's enormous and legendary All-American lineman in the early 1900s.*

last minute 60-yard punt by Chicago's Walter Eckersall and subsequent safety brought the Maroons a two-point victory – Michigan's first defeat in a staggering 57 games. Graduation would soon decimate the Wolverine attack. So Yost set about creating a new one.

As he looked back on that phenomenal four-year run, Yost reflected with pride on the innovative plays his teams had introduced or adapted to their own style. He told famous sportswriter Grantland Rice: "In 1901, we used spinners, reverses, double reverses, laterals, split backs – everything that is in the modern game except the forward pass."

In putting together a new Wolverine team around Adolph "Germany" Schulz, Yost proved that even he was open to suggestion. Schulz was football's first behind-the-line center; he felt that dropping back as each scrimmage began gave him a better view of the field. After initial objections, Yost adopted Schulz' idea – first obtaining the youth's promise that if any opposing player got by him, he would return to the line. The next few years would prove that very few players got by the 6-foot, 4-inch, 245-pound Schulz.

However, beating opposing teams was not the only thing on Fielding Yost's mind in 1906. A conference convened by Michigan President James Angell passed several new rules regarding the administration of Western Conference football programs. Among the new rules passed were the prohibition of the training table, a limit of three years of football eligibility, and a maximum of five games, which would in effect mean that Michigan would have to

cut short its strong rivalries with Eastern opponents.

The eligibility rule was also onerous to Coach Yost. It was intended to be retroactive, which would have meant that Michigan's seniors would have to sit out their final season.

Michigan's Board in Control asked for several modifications to the rules, among them a seven-game schedule and repeal of the retroactive three-year eligibility limit. After two years of frustration and delays,

Above: *Michigan Captain Allerdice punts from his own goal line at Philadelphia's Franklin Field in 1909. Michigan beat Penn 12-6.*

Michigan's modification proposals were rejected at the Western Conference meeting of January 4, 1908. On February 1 the University of Michigan officially left the conference.

Such was the strength of Michigan's program and established rivalries that for a time the Wolverines went on as if nothing had changed. With the forward pass now legal, a six-man line was a decided advantage. Michigan had gone 4-1 in 1906 for a share of the conference title, even as it fought the new regulations. In 1907 the team was unscored upon, racking up 107 points in five shutouts, only to lose 6-0 to Penn in the season finale. Germany Schulz was named an All-American for 1907. With home games taking place in Michigan's new Ferry Field, with a seating capacity of 18,000, fan interest was as high as ever.

A game with Minnesota and their "Minnesota Shift" in 1910 at Ferry Field proved one of the barnburners of the decade as it demonstrated the benefit of a strong passing game. Minnesota's Shift, in which they lined up in one formation, then quickly shifted to another and snapped the ball, had crushed six straight opponents for Dr. Henry Williams' team, and Michigan's 1910 team was not one of its strongest. But Yost thought he had a way to counter the Shift.

He taught his tackles how to shift with Minnesota, matching power with power. Neither team could gain an advantage and there was no score with six minutes left on the clock. Then Yost unveiled a shift of his own, with All-American Stan Wells shifting at the last minute from his right end

position to the backfield. Wells took the snap and threw a pass for 30 yards. Then he did it again, on almost the same play. Michigan was calling no plays and lining up immediately. The Minnesota line temporarily stopped further advance, until tackle Al Benbrook, a massive 6-foot, 5-inch, 265-pound lineman, suggested Wells follow him with the ball. He barreled into the Minnesota line with Wells sprinting after him to cross the goal line. Michigan had scored a 6-0 victory using brilliant passing to gain yardage – three years before Knute Rockne and Gus Dorais popularized the pass for Notre Dame.

Banned from conference play after that 1910 game with Minnesota, Yost and the Wolverines concentrated on their Eastern rivals. Through the years from 1910 to 1917, having games with schools like Penn kept Michigan football in front of national fans and made up for other dates with schools like Mount Union, Marietta and Lawrence. It also brought outstanding Wolverine players the press they needed to become All-Americans.

Halfback Jimmy Craig was one of them. In a game against Penn in 1911, Craig sprinted down the field after the Penn line had fallen prey to one of Yost's shifts, scoring the winning touchdown.

Johnny Maulbetsch was another. Just 5 feet, 7 inches tall and 153 pounds, he plowed his way through a Harvard defense in 1914 for 133 yards in 30 rushes, gaining more yardage than the entire Harvard backfield put together. Michigan lost the game 7-0, but later author Ring Lardner wrote:

"After this, if any Easterner tells you that the game played back East is superior to that played in the Midwest, try not to laugh yourself to death. Johnny Maulbetsch of Michigan shot that theory full of holes."

Maulbetsch made All-America as a sophomore, but went on for two more seasons at Michigan with such desire and purpose that a trophy is awarded in his name. It goes to the freshman who exhibits the character, leadership and desire he became famous for. In a somewhat depressing era for the Wolverine football program, Maulbetsch captured the hearts of the Michigan fans. Songwriter and poet Fred Lawton put his feelings about Maulbetsch into words:

He didn't make the touchdown,
And we didn't win the game,
But little Johnny Maulbetsch
Led the Wolverines to fame.
For, in those glorious minutes,
When young Mauly gave his all,
We learned of Michigan spirit
From his words, "GIMME DA BALL!"
His spirit burst into a flame
When victory hopes were slim,
The "Victors" and the "Varsity"
Became a part of him!
You ask the meaning of this
Michigan spirit – yours and mine?
Just think of Johnny Maulbetsch
When he hit that Harvard line!

Above: *Pint-sized Johnny Maulbetsch starred in the Harvard game in 1914, inspiring poet and songwriter Fred Lawton to immortalize him in verse.*

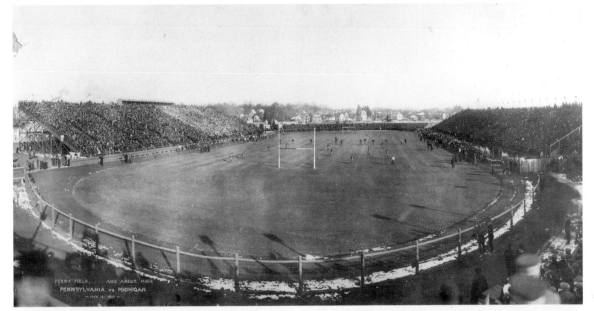

Left: *Michigan's Ferry Field as it looked during the 1907 Penn game.*

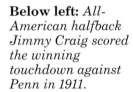

Below far left: *Stanfield Wells helped win the 1910 Minnesota game 6-0, with the forward pass.*

Below left: *All-American halfback Jimmy Craig scored the winning touchdown against Penn in 1911.*

Above: *A player practicing with a rudimentary tackling dummy in 1914, as Yost oversees.*

Michigan took six victories from a schedule of nine games in the 1914 season, with Maulbetsch tallying 12 touchdowns and Tommy Hughitt calling the signals.

But the following season, 1915, was a disappointment as the Wolverines lost three of seven games. It seemed that although there were moments of glory, and good individual efforts, Yost could not find the stuff with which to build a cohesive, winning team.

And there was something else: Michigan fans, alumni and even some faculty members were beginning to regret leaving the conference. Games with Cornell and Penn provided some excitement each season, but they could not replace the thrilling and enduring rivalries with Minnesota, Wisconsin and Chicago.

Still, the 1916 season, with Johnny Maulbetsch now a senior and captain of the Wolverines, saw Michigan tally seven straight wins before going down to defeat at the hands of both Penn and Cornell. During a 1916 game with Michigan Agricultural College (soon to be renamed Michigan State University), a freaky play occurred which is still remembered. Yost's new quarterback, Cliff Sparks, who was playing in one of his first games, readied himself to hold the snap for Maulbetsch's field goal attempt from the 32. As the fans watched, the snap sailed high over Sparks' head. Quick as a flash he leaped up to grab it, then coolly drop kicked a perfect field goal!

As these gridiron heroics were taking place, a movement was afoot behind the scenes. Law Professor Ralph Aigler, who had been appointed to the Board in Control of Athletics in 1913, began to rally support on the Board for Michigan's return to the Western Conference. When Aigler was made Chairman of the Board in 1915, he swiftly began asking other faculty representatives around the conference how they would feel about Michigan's return to the fold. Reaction was favorable, but first Michigan would have to assure the conference brass that the school's faculty had a firm grip on the athletic programs.

Aigler had some diplomatic work to do at home as well. Detroit alumni were anti-conference, and athletic director Phil Bartelme was also initially opposed. However, the grind of putting together seven to ten football dates per season began to change Bartelme's view on the subject. In the fall of 1916 he remarked to Aigler, "I am getting tired of begging for games to fill out our schedule. Michigan ought not to have to do that. I believe the thing to do is to get back to our own group, and that means joining the conference."

With Bartelme on his side (probably he was strongly influenced by Yost), Aigler felt the tide had turned. The majority of Wolverine alumni clamored for a return to the conference, and in April of 1917 Aigler arranged for the Regents to vote on a new resolution allowing the University Senate to have veto power over the actions of the Board in Control of Athletics.

This action had the effect of proving that Michigan football was controlled by the faculty of the university. In addition, Michigan agreed to abolish its training table. They applied to the Western Conference for re-admission in time to play Northwestern on November 20, 1917. No doubt breathing a sigh of relief, the conference granted the request. At last – Michigan was back!

As World War I cast a shadow over college football and several star players transferred to service teams or were sent overseas, Coach Fielding Yost still had reason to feel satisfied. The Wolverines' 10-year record outside the conference was a laudable 52-16-7, even though no championships had come their way.

But now they were back in the Midwestern "family," and the conference soon adopted the name by which they were often called and which Michigan's re-entry made official – The Big-10.

Above: *Law Professor Ralph Aigler helped bring Michigan back to the Western Conference in 1917.*

Left: *Quarterback Harold Zeiger makes a 30-yard run against Cornell in Ithaca in November of 1916.*

3. Path to Glory 1918-1926

The level of college play during the war dropped dramatically nationwide, and the Big-10 was no exception. Fielding Yost's Wolverines lost that initial contest with Northwestern but then racked up eight victories. Three Wolverine players made the All-America list that year: fullback Cedric Smith, Ernest Allmendinger and Frank Culver.

The 1918 season was even better, as Michigan's passing plays found success against the decimated squads of the Big Ten. One of the reasons for Michigan's winning ways was tackle Angus Goetz. A whiz at scoring off of defensive interceptions and fumble recoveries, he was headed for a medical career and had nearly quit the

team at the start of the season to pursue his medical studies full-time. While sympathizing with his player's desire to be of service during wartime (a flu epidemic was also raging in the U.S.), Yost had used his considerable powers of persuasion to talk Goetz into remaining with the Wolverines. Goetz would become the first player under Yost to captain the squad twice, in both the 1919 and 1920 seasons.

Highlights of the 1918 season included a 13-0 win over the Chicago Maroons, during which Goetz ran a blocked field goal 50 yards for a touchdown, and a 21-6 victory over Michigan Agricultural College. Goetz picked up a fumble and scored during that game as well. Other 1918 standouts were

Below: Michigan fans form a block M in the Ferry Field stands during a game in 1914.

All-American fullback Frank Steketee and center Ernie Vick.

A post-season game with Illinois would have been the only way to determine a conference champion that season, and Illinois refused such an offer. Michigan press reports hinted that the Illini might have cold feet – eliciting a haughty response from fiery Illini coach Bob Zuppke. "Michigan's record the last 10 years is not awe-inspiring enough to give anyone cold feet." It was obvious that here was a Big Ten member who was not thrilled about Michigan's return. These and other comments in the press started a feud between Zuppke and Yost that simmered for years.

During the 1919 season Yost's wartime luck ran out and the Wolverines posted a disappointing 3-4 mark – Yost's worst season record. His squad was fragmented by service demands and the ineligibility of Steketee. For perhaps the first time, students and alumni began to criticize Yost, asking whether he'd lost his touch. The Wolverine coach went on the offensive, asking not for patience or indulgence, but for more players and more Michigan spirit.

He soon had to rein in overzealous alumni, who were searching out potential players in every corner of the land. Fra-ternity memos like this one were circulated before the Christmas break: "Your duty is to talk Michigan and search out all available prospects in your local area during Christmas vacation." Michigan alumni power was mobilized. It may not have helped with the immediate manpower problem, but it did insure that when the servicemen returned, the name of the University of Michigan was one they revered.

The 1920 season heralded the beginning of end Paul Goebel's career as a Wolverine. A talented engineering student, he could also pass the football, and he would captain the 1922 squad. Steketee was back, and Frank "Cappie" Cappon joined the varsity. With captain Goetz at tackle, the Wolverines looked strong again. They managed five wins but lost to hated Illinois for a second straight year, and also to eventual conference champ Ohio State. A highlight was their 14-0 win over Chicago. Playing on that 1920 Maroon squad was a young man who would later become a legend of Michigan athletics: Herbert O. "Fritz" Crisler.

Despite the two setbacks, prospects for 1921 looked bright. Vick and Goebel were back, and they were joined by a pint-sized package of triple-threat power in Harry Kipke. Weighing only 158 pounds and

Below: *A display of Michigan punters in 1922. The great Michigan halfback and future Wolverine coach Harry Kipke is at center.*

MICHIGAN'S PUNTERS

standing only 5 feet 9 inches, he had nevertheless become a sensation at Lansing High by doing it all – running, passing, punting and catching the football. He seemed born for Michigan football, and he would be joined by Doug Roby from hotbed Holland, Michigan, and Bernie Kirk, a fine athlete and prized transferee from Notre Dame.

Something else had changed as the Wolverines headed into that exciting season. Athletic Director Phil Bartelme had abruptly resigned, and Fielding Yost was now A.D. as well as volunteer unpaid football coach.

Right: *Captain Harry Kipke helped "dedicate" Ohio State's new stadium with a 19-0 victory in 1922. Kipke's 11 punts in the game averaged 47 yards.*

With Kipke thrilling the fans with his running and kicking, Michigan began the season with three straight shutouts. Ohio State loomed, and a Ferry Field crowd of 45,000 showed up to root for another win. An early exit for Kipke due to injury proved an ill omen, however, and the Buckeyes won, 14-0.

As so often happens after a disappointing loss, the critics and second-guessers came out of the woodwork. A *Michigan Daily* headline over a letter to the editor declared, "Yost Has Seen His Day."

The following week the Wolverines beat Illinois 3-0 on a Steketee field goal and the boos subsided somewhat. Next up were the powerful Badgers of Wisconsin, and Michigan was given little chance of winning.

Yost, feeling his authority and prestige eroding somewhat, wanted this victory badly, and from all accounts gave one of his most emotional pre-game speeches. He followed it up by trying some innovative plays from the past – among them the Minnesota end back play.

End Goebel dropped into the backfield, caught a lateral pass and lobbed it downfield to Doug Roby for a touchdown. The game ended in a 7-7 tie – not good enough for Yost.

The next weekend saw the Wolverines drub Minnesota's Golden Gophers 38-0 to finish the season with 5-1-1 record. Even as the Iowa Hawkeyes were crowned Big-10 champions, Yost was pondering the improvements he would need to make in the off-season. For the glory of Michigan, and for the sake of his own prestige, he was determined to be back on top.

The highlight of the 1922 Big-10 season would be the opening of Ohio's State's huge new stadium. Holding over 72,000 fans, it was the largest football facility west of the Yale Bowl. Buckeye fans felt that a fourth straight victory over the Wolverines would be a fitting dedication for the new stadium. Coach Yost and the irrepressible Harry Kipke had other plans.

Leading 3-0 on a Goebel field goal in the first quarter, the Wolverines moved slowly but surely down to Ohio State's 34 late in the first half. Quarterback Irwin Uteritz took the snap, started right and faked a handoff to an end. Then he sent a shovel pass into the arms of a lightning quick Kipke, who had faked right, then whirled left, leaving two Buckeye defenders grabbing empty air.

As Ohio State fans gasped in horror, Kipke danced across the goal line. Then he tossed the ball to an official and quipped, "Well, the place is really dedicated now!"

It was Yost's "Old 83" play, and that touchdown was only the most famous of the

Left: *Fielding Yost in his final years as Michigan's greatest football coach. His 1920s teams were among his best.*

Below: *A diagram of Yost's famous "Old 83" play, used by Harry Kipke to score the first touchdown ever made in Ohio Stadium.*

several Wolverine tallies resulting from it over the years. Kipke scored another touchdown with a 45-yard run, then drop kicked a field goal to pace Michigan in their 19-0 "dedication."

After the game, no less an authority than Walter Camp took him aside and said, "Kipke, you're the greatest punter in football history." His 11 punts in the OSU game had averaged 47 yards.

The Wolverines were on a roll, pasting Illinois 24-0, crushing Michigan State 63-0, and edging Wisconsin and Minnesota by scores of 13-6 and 16-7 respectively. All criticism of Yost faded away. Michigan's only blemish on that season was a scoreless tie with Vanderbilt. Unfortunately, Iowa was having one of its best seasons ever under Coach Howard Harding Jones, and the Wolverines had to settle once again for a shared Big-10 crown.

Both Goebel and Kipke were named All-Americans. Tragically, Bernie Kirk's selec-

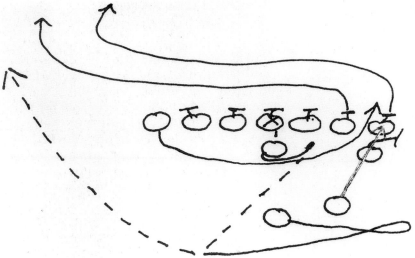

tion as a second-team All-American was told to him as he lay in a hospital bed, dying from meningitis resulting from a car accident. He died five days after the incident.

As the 1923 season kicked off, Michigan's

Right: *Harry Kipke shows his kicking prowess to Coach Yost during a practice session in 1922.*

undefeated string mounted. After easy non-conference victories over Case and Vanderbilt, the Wolverines delighted a packed crowd at Ferry Field (tickets sold for up to $50 each) with a 23-0 routing of the Buckeyes. A 9-3 escape from mighty Iowa fanned hopes for a title of Michigan's own that year, but the squad was banged up and bruised. Three starters were out of the lineup, including quarterback Uteritz with a broken leg.

By the time the yearly battle with Wisconsin loomed, Yost must have wondered whether he had enough healthy bodies for a shot at the victory. That epic contest at Wisconsin's Camp Randall Field, which ended in a 6-3 victory for Michigan, nearly cost the referee his life.

Respected referee Walter Eckersall, a former Chicago star, had ruled a Michigan

touchdown in the second quarter, when many Wisconsin fans thought Wolverine ball-carrier Tod Rockwell had stepped out of bounds.

The second half was a nail-biter, with Michigan clinging to a 6-3 lead. Wisconsin players knew their only hope was a long pass. Badger fullback Taft let go a long one, and in the ensuing seconds it was caught by a Badger end, fumbled, and picked up by a Wisconsin halfback. As Badger Harris charged for Michigan's goal, Butch Slaughter dove for him and dragged him to the ground at the 15-yard line. A few moments later time ran out and the Wolverines had preserved the 6-3 victory.

Wisconsin fans stormed the field, headed for Eckersall, whom they blamed for the earlier Wolverine score. Only the cool head of Badger captain Marty Below, who with a few teammates surrounded Eckersall and escorted him off the field, saved the referee from the revenge of the mob.

Michigan topped off its fine 1923 season with a 10-0 win over Minnesota, but the Wolverines again accepted only a share of the conference title – this time they split it with the Illini. The end of their college playing days had come for both Paul Goebel and Harry Kipke, but neither, in a real sense, ever left Michigan. Kipke would return to coach, and Goebel became Mayor of Grand Rapids, a Michigan Regent, and a lifelong supporter of the University.

Despite recent successes, there had been persistent rumors about Yost's retirement from coaching. For the 1924 season he installed a new football coach, George Little, from football hotbed Miami University of Ohio. The biggest game of that season was to be the "dedication game" for the University of Illinois' new stadium.

Arch-rival Illinois would not only open the new facility against the Wolverines –

they would use the occasion to showcase the greatest football star in their history: Red Grange. It was quite possibly the most eagerly anticipated college football game in history.

Harry L. Farrell, sportswriter for the United Press in New York, described the anticipation: "Out here in the West, where men are men and football teams are made of them, nobody wants to discuss anything but the battle impending between Michigan and Illinois. More than 70,000 spectators are expected, and double that number of seats could have been sold if there were places for that number. There is more real enthusiasm around here than there has been in New Haven or Boston for the Harvard-Yale games."

Yost and Little were hardly helpless in preparing for Grange. Though they had lost Kipke and Jack Blott, they had captain Herb Steger, who could kick and run, and other fine returning lettermen. But they had little idea of what they were in for. In

Below: *Wolverine Captain Herb Steger powers through the Illinois line at Champaign during the famous 1924 game. That game is best remembered for the legendary Harold "Red" Grange's five touchdowns, scored against Michigan in Illinois' dedication game.*

Below: *Coach Yost in uniform poses in 1926 with his quarterback, Benny Friedman, who was to team up with Bennie Oosterbaan in the famous "Benny-to-Bennie" passing attack.*

front of a packed crowd in the new facility at Champaign on October 18, 1924, the Wolverines took the field against Red Grange and the Fighting Illini.

Grange, wearing number 77, returned Steger's opening kickoff 95 yards for a touchdown, and followed it up with three more TDs the next three times he held the football, on runs of 67, 56 and 44 yards. It

must have been a triumphant afternoon indeed for Illini Coach Bob Zuppke, who had labored in relative obscurity until the day Harold Grange had come out for football.

After Illinois took a 27-0 lead in the first 12 minutes of the game, Zuppke held Grange out until the second half, when he returned to score a fifth TD.

Michigan went down to a 39-14 defeat,

Below: Coach Yost in uniform poses in 1926 with his quarterback, Benny Friedman, who was to team up with Bennie Oosterbaan in the famous "Benny-to-Bennie" passing attack.

but they did have Steger's exploits to cheer. The Michigan captain, playing without a helmet, charged again and again into the Illini line, scoring the final touchdown. The Wolverines gave it their all, but were beaten by a superior team. Such was the public and press attention given to this game that Red Grange's exploits as the "Galloping Ghost" became the stuff of legend. Even seasoned Big-10 observers had underestimated the abilities of the shy redhead until his singlehanded drubbing of the Wolverines.

Behind the scenes, as the defeated team headed back to Ann Arbor, all was far from quiet. Yost and his wife Eunice had been helpless witnesses in the stands at the Illinois game, and Yost decided to take over preparations for the next game, against Wisconsin. He made a few changes; one of them was to start benchwarmer Benny Friedman at right halfback. The sophomore had thrown a couple of passes late in the Illinois game – an inauspicious beginning to what was to be a brilliant Wolverine career.

Friedman figured prominently in a decisive 21-0 win over the Badgers. Although Iowa upset Michigan 9-2 in the final game, and the conference crown went to Chicago that year, Friedman would be back.

But George Little would not. Recognizing the obvious, that Yost still considered himself in charge of Wolverine football, Little left Michigan for Wisconsin. There he assumed the duties of athletic director and football coach.

Meanwhile, Yost reinstalled himself as coach, but added some fresh blood to his brain trust: returning alumni Cappie Cappon, Jack Blott and, fresh from Missouri, Harry Kipke. Some promising sophomores would join the varsity for the fall of 1925. Better days were coming!

It is not recorded exactly when Benny Friedman first threw a pass to big blond Bennie Oosterbaan in practice – but Yost must have liked what he saw, because the Wolverines started off the 1925 season with five straight shutouts. With the "Benny to Bennie" passing combination confounding opposing defenses, Michigan beat Michigan State 39-0, Indiana 63-0, Little-

1926 MICHIGAN FOOTBALL COACHING STAFF.
L-R: Coach Yost, Trainer Hoyt, E. E. Wieman, C. P. Kean, J. L. Blott, H. G. Kipke, G. Veenker, R. L. Holle and E. J. Mather.

Above: *Michigan's coaching staff, led by Fielding Yost (left), prior to the Navy game in 1926.*

Left: *Benny Friedman in a classic pose. He was the greatest quarterback in the first 100 years of Michigan football.*

Above: *Wolverine Bob Brown keeps "Galloping Ghost" Red Grange from getting to the ball carrier during the Illinois game in 1925.*

coached Wisconsin 21-0, Illinois 3-0 and Navy 54-0.

Only a rain-soaked loss to Northwestern marred their record before the Wolverines beat OSU 10-0 and finished off the season by stomping on the Gophers 35-0.

Benny Friedman later recalled the Wisconsin win as a particularly satisfying one for him. "It was Yost who prevailed on Little to start me after that Red Grange holocaust," he recalled. "I could not play quarterback for Coach Little, because I did not personify what he wanted. Now, under Yost, I was the quarterback, and this game meant much to me."

Yost, a battle-scarred veteran of so many Michigan campaigns, called his 1925 squad "the finest I ever coached." These Wolverines, none of whom weighed over 200 pounds, had scored 227 points and allowed only 3 that season. They claimed their 10th conference championship, and were acknowledged by most sportswriters to be the nation's finest team.

Friedman and Oosterbaan were accorded All-America status, along with Tom Edwards, guard Harry Hawkins and linebacker Bob Brown. Friedman had passed for 760 yards and 14 touchdowns.

Flush with success, Yost threw himself into plans for a new stadium seating up to 80,000 students, and made arrangements with Coach Doc Spears of Minnesota for the Wolverines and the Gophers to play not once but twice during the 1926 season.

Quarterback Friedman, no doubt recalling many crunching Gopher tackles of the past, was not enthusiastic. "It's alright, Ben," Yost supposedly told him. "We'll outsmart them."

"That's okay for you, coach," retorted Friedman. "But you don't have to play against those guys."

Yost felt the Wolverines were headed for a big season with Friedman calling the signals, and with Oosterbaan and fullback Wally Weber in the backfield – and he was right. In the opening game against Oklahoma A & M (coached by former Wolverine All-American Johnny Maulbetsch), Friedman threw three passes for touchdowns to back Bo Molenda and another to Oosterbaan for a 42-3 laugher. Next, MSU fell to the Wolverine passing machine, 55-3.

Navy slowed down the juggernaut with a 10-0 victory in front of 80,000 football-crazed fans in Baltimore – a game that saw some serious manhandling of QB Friedman by Navy's enormous tackles. At one point he turned to his friend and touchdown partner, Oosterbaan, and suggested *he* try passing for a change. Oosterbaan wound up in a pile of Navy defenders.

"When we pried him loose," recalled Friedman, "Oosterbaan looked at me and said, 'If it's all the same to you, Benny, I'd rather catch passes than throw them.'"

Back on track the next week in a win over Wisconsin, the Michigan squad looked ahead to an all-important date with the Ohio State Buckeyes. More than 90,000 fans turned out in Columbus' expanded stadium to watch the game. They were in for a treat – although perhaps not the kind they expected.

The Buckeyes' idea of a warm welcome for the Wolverines was to score 10 points in the first 12 minutes of the contest. During a timeout, Weber turned to Oosterbaan and said, "Ben, at this rate they're going to beat us 40-0." To which the irrepressible Oosterbaan replied with a grin, "Dammit, Wally, we haven't had the ball yet."

Indeed. A short time later Friedman hurled a bullet to Oosterbaan on the OSU 21, then faked a place-kick formation and threw another bullet to the handy end, who was parked in the Buckeye end zone.

With 30 seconds left in the first half, the Wolverines again assumed a place-kick pattern – but Oosterbaan whispered a few words to the QB. Immediately the Buckeyes smelled another trick play and yelled to each other, "Fake! Fake! Watch Oosterbaan!" The Ohio State line parted for Friedman like the Red Sea, and he proceeded to kick a perfect 44-yard field goal to tie the game at 10-10.

When asked later what he had said, Oosterbaan flashed his trademark grin and replied, "I merely asked Louie Gilbert, who was the holder, 'Isn't this a long way to kick a ball, Louie?'"

In the fourth period Wolverine Sid Dewey recovered an OSU fumble, and Michigan made it pay off with another Friedman touchdown pass – this time to Leo Hoffman, for a sweet 17-16 win.

But Oosterbaan's best game came the following week, during a grind-it-out barnburner against Minnesota in "Game 2" of the season series (the Wolverines had won the opener 20-0). The field was frozen and Yost had run his troops through a special drill wherein they practiced grabbing the pigskin off the frozen turf.

Although the Gophers came out storming, scoring in the second quarter and reeling off first downs against the visitors, Yost's team tightened their chinstraps and waited for their break. It came in the fourth quarter, when the Gophers fumbled on their own 40. Oosterbaan's nose for the football allowed him to plow through the line and scoop up the ball. Afraid to look back, he charged 60 yards for the TD. "Every step I took I kept thinking, 'Won't I look like a chump if somebody catches me from behind?' I guess that made me run faster." The result was a 7-6 win for the good guys.

After the game Yost quipped, "It's not the first downs that count, y'know, it's the touchdowns." Another shared title, this time with Northwestern's Wildcats, cheered Michigan fans even as it signaled the end of an era.

Below: *Benny Friedman (left), Fielding Yost and Bennie Oosterbaan in 1926. Together they formed the nucleus of Michigan's great teams of the 1920s.*

Friedman had played his last game for the school he loved. Before going on to pro football and college coaching, the handsome QB again garnered All-America honors with Oosterbaan. They were the first passing pair in college football history to win consecutive honors – and it was also the first time in the history of official All-America selections that no players from "The Big Three" of Harvard, Yale and Princeton were chosen.

It was the end of the Yost era too. The craggy coach wanted to devote all his considerable energies to the construction of the new Michigan stadium. He dreamed of it being the finest athletic facility in the nation, and under his care it would be. While he left open the possibility of coaching again someday, he wanted his top assistant and crack recruiter Elton "Tad" Wieman to take over the coaching reins. He would remain a tireless after-dinner speaker, athletic director, and die-hard fan of Michigan.

His players remembered him with fondness. His pre-game speeches, his impromptu meetings with players, which included lectures on playing their position, had all become part of the legend. Yost's brain, and mouth, were always working.

"Who are they to try to beat a Meeshegan team?" he would bellow into the silence of the pre-game locker room. "They're only human. You're the Wolverines!"

Perhaps sportswriter Ring Lardner best described Yost's irrepressible nature and constant stream of chatter. When asked if he had ever spoken with Yost, he replied, "No, I didn't. My father taught me never to interrupt."

Right: *Louie Gilbert led Michigan's ground game against Ohio-Wesleyan in 1928.*

Left: *Some of the greatest legends in sports gathered prior to a dinner in 1925. Left to right: Glenn "Pop" Warner, who coached at Cornell, Carlisle, Pitt, Stanford and Temple; Notre Dame Coach Knute Rockne; Yankee immortal Babe Ruth; Christy Walsh, head of an All-America board; Tad Jones, a great Yale coach; and Coach Fielding Yost of Michigan.*

Left: *Fielding H. Yost poses with a statue of the Michigan wolverine. "Hurry Up" Yost retired from coaching in 1926, leaving behind a 165-29 record after 25 years at the helm.*

4. A New Era 1927-1950

In his first year as coach, Tad Wieman benefited from Oosterbaan's fine senior year and the excellent work of Louie Gilbert in the backfield as Friedman's passing successor. Michigan compiled a 6-2 season with five shutouts and a single conference loss to eventual national champion Illinois. Oosterbaan became an All-American for the third straight time. He was the only Wolverine ever to be so honored. What many football fans didn't know was that he was also an All-American at another thriving college sport – basketball. To top it off he had led the Big-10 in hitting on the baseball team. The nine-letter Wolverine stayed around after graduation to help coach both basketball and football – but he was lost to Wieman on the field.

Another highlight of that 1927 season had been the dedication of Yost's dream stadium. Originally designed to hold 72,000, Yost had campaigned for another "tempor-

Left: *Michigan Stadium as it looked in 1929 during the Harvard game, when the Wolverines defeated Harvard for the first time. The stadium now seats more than 100,000 fans.*

Left: *Harry Newman was Coach Kipke's passing star in 1930.*

ary" 10,000 wooden seats. Gradually, of course, these and other temporary seats would become permanent parts of today's Michigan Stadium, which holds over 100,000 spectators.

Yost was in his glory that October day against (who else) Ohio State when the place was formally dedicated. More than 84,000 fans yelled themselves hoarse as the Governors of Ohio and Michigan walked with Yost across the field. Later, and perhaps more importantly, Oosterbaan's pinpoint passing to Louie Gilbert insured a 21-0 win.

However, the following season, 1928, was dismal. Although All-American tackle Otto Pommerening provided some fan thrills, a 3-4-1 mark guaranteed Wieman's swift exit as coach. Yost installed his old star halfback, Harry Kipke, as the new Wolverine football coach – prying him loose from his coaching job at Michigan State, where they hated to see him go. It would prove to be a sound decision on Yost's part.

Throughout the 1929 rebuilding year, the no-nonsense Kipke stressed fundamentals: kicking, passing and defense were practiced over and over until perfect. The Wolverines' 5-3-1 record that year included Michigan's first-ever win over Harvard, and a hard-fought, victorious battle for the Little Brown Jug against the Minnesota Gophers and Bronko Nagurski. But Kipke's sights were set much higher. He had a new passing combo joining his varsity that he was itching to try: Harry Newman and Ivy Williamson. Some talented freshmen had caught his eye, too – among them a

kid named Francis Wistert. Better days were coming.

They came indeed. During the 1930 season Newman became an instant star at quarterback, passing brilliantly and pacing the team to an 8-0-1 year and a share of the Big-10 title, with only a scoreless tie against MSU to mar the season. Kipke had held Newman out until the third game of the 1930 season, inexplicably. Once Newman got his chance he earned a starting job for the following two seasons, despite an ankle injury that hobbled him during the 1931 season. That year the Wolverines posted an 8-1-1 mark and a three-way share of the conference crown with Northwestern and Purdue.

A footnote to the 1931 season was an invitation to the reinstituted Rose Bowl in Pasadena: it was politely declined in keeping with the Big-10's prohibition on postseason games.

Along the way the team was rebuilding pride and confidence, and was featuring some star players. Center Maynard Morrison was named an All-American after the 1930 season. Ted Petoskey, an end, and tackle Chuck Bernard were named All-Americans along with Harry Newman in 1932, a stellar year in the history of Michigan football.

It was based on dedication and spirit. Ted Petoskey described the kind of confidence the team had in its own abilities: "We were never afraid to give the other team the ball. We always figured when we wanted the ball, we could take it from them. We took pride in holding our opponents for negative yardage. We never considered missing practice. It just never crossed our minds. We had a job to do that we loved, and we loved to do our job." What coach wouldn't be successful with such players?

Above: *All-American Wolverine Chuck Bernard poses in 1932.*

Right: *The 1932 Wolverine squad. Captain Ivan "Ivy" Williamson is flanked by Coach Kipke and Athletic Director Yost in Kipke's second Big-10 Championship team. This team scored 123 points against their opponents on their way to an 8-0 season, while only 13 points were scored against them.*

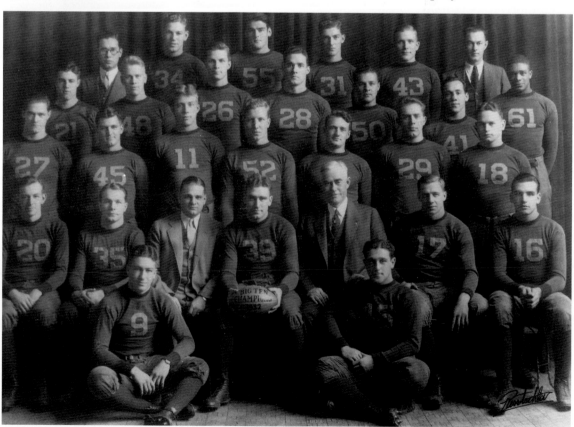

In the 1932 season this team spirit flowered and enabled the Michigan squad to roll over eight straight opponents – holding six scoreless, using plays like quarterback sneaks and 78-yard punt returns, and winning the Big-10 title and the national championship outright. Along the way they earned praise across the land, although critics still described their offense as consisting of "a punt, a pass, and a prayer."

The following season Bernard and Petoskey were both back, and Francis Wistert, now a sophomore tackle, began to turn heads. He and his two brothers, Albert and Alvin, would all make All-America at Michigan, but in 1933 Francis "Whitey" Wistert only knew that he was playing in his first game for the Wolverines against Illinois, and he was scared. Senior Stan Hozer, right guard, gave the youngster some encouragement any first-year player would like to have.

"Look, kid," he said. "All you have to do is lean against me on every play, and keep that Illinois guard from falling off my shoulder when I block him."

Francis, to be followed by Albert and Alvin, became an All-American tackle for Michigan, wearing the number 11. He would later be chosen Big-10 MVP in baseball and sign a pro contract with the Cincinnati Reds. The 1933 season was another good one for the Wolverines, as they chalked up a 7-0-1 season and a second national title in a row – only a tie with the pesky Golden Gophers spoiled perfection. Kipke had put together 22 straight wins,

and a gaudy four-year record of 31-1-3.

But graduation was to prove Kipke's undoing. He lost most of the core of that great team, and the next four seasons (1934-1937) proved one of the most depressing periods in the history of Wolverine football. Records of 1-7, 4-4, 1-7 and 4-4, and no Michigan All-Americans, tried alumni patience. It was during this bleak period that a feisty center named Gerry Ford earned 1934 MVP honors from his teammates before starting a political career that ended in the White House.

Later Ford would recall his days at Michigan, especially a hard-fought 34-0 loss against heavily-favored Minnesota in 1934: "During 25 years in the rough-and-tumble world of politics, I often thought of the experiences before, during and after

Above left: *Center (later U.S. President) Gerald Ford in the 1933 game against Cornell.*

Above: *Francis "Whitey" Wistert, shown here in 1933, was the first of three brothers to be named All-American as tackle for Michigan – all wearing number 11.*

Left: *Wolverine captain Joe Rinaldi in 1937 (holding ball) flanked by Coach Hunk Anderson, Head Coach Harry Kipke and long-time and beloved Assistant Coach Wally Weber.*

Right: *Captain Forrest Evashevski clears a path for Tom Harmon as the 1940 football season gets underway. This devastating combination led Michigan to an almost undefeated season that year, marred only by a loss to Minnesota.*

Below: *All-American guard Ralph Heikkinen in 1937.*

that game in 1934. Remembering them has helped me many times to face a tough situation, take action, and make every effort possible despite adverse odds. I remember how Michigan students and people in Ann Arbor met us at the train station that Sunday. There was a rousing parade, and this was a meaningful tribute to the fight the Wolverines had put up against Minnesota."

Eventually, of course, Yost's patience ran out and he replaced Kipke as Wolverine football coach. He knew who he wanted to be Michigan's new coach – Herbert "Fritz" Crisler, who had coached under Stagg at Chicago, and been an innovator for two years at Minnesota. But how to pry him away from Princeton, where he had done much to turn around a losing program? Eventually the thoughtful, articulate Crisler was promised the athletic director's job when Yost planned to retire in three years. He also received an unprecedented salary and power over Michigan athletic programs. Perhaps most important to his future success, Crisler had the incredible luck and timing to inherit from Kipke two promising sophomores whom he would start in 1938: Forrest Evashevski and Tom Harmon.

Kipke probably knew his 1937 freshmen were something special when his varsity had difficulty beating them during a scrimmage. Besides Evashevski and Harmon,

the 1938 sophomores included Paul Kromer and Howard Mehaffey from Ohio's Kiski Prep, guard Ralph Fritz, and a friend of Harmon's from Gary, Indiana – Ed Christy.

Harmon himself was hardly a "dark horse" – he had earned 14 letters in four sports at Horace Mann High School. But Michigan football was to make him a star, and a man. From his freshman year to his graduation, he would grow from 145 to 195 pounds. But his head never got too big. Harmon, with help from his buddy and teammate "Evy" Evashevski, managed to live life as a young man while the rest of the football world eagerly tried to turn him into a god.

Wolverine football was ready for a superstar. With a strong heritage of star coaches and cohesive team play, few Michigan players had emerged from the group to dazzle the fans. But one look at Thomas Dudley Harmon, number 98, in his starting debut against Chicago, and Crisler knew this kid was different.

In a strong 1938 season during which Michigan went 6-1-1 – losing only to Minnesota, with "vest pocket" guard Ralph Heikkinen an All-American – the highlight was still Harmon's play. Beginning with a 59-yard touchdown sprint against the Maroons, and continuing with a touchdown run and a pass to Evy for another against the Illini, Harmon seemed to have a private, magic relationship with the football. It did his bidding, apparently without effort.

The 1939 season debuted with few but the football-wise knowing who the talkative Irishman was. The fans would soon learn. Eventually a tailback, Harmon was still at right halfback in Crisler's offense as the Wolverines knocked off MSU 26-13, with Evy and Bob Westfall supplying the running power. Then, against Iowa and the great Nile Kinnick, Harmon let loose with all of Michigan's points, including a touchdown on a 95-yard pass interception, for a 27-7 win. Next was an 85-0 romp over the Maroons, who were in their final season of intercollegiate football. Harmon scored 21 points against Yale, and gained 203 yards in a game against Penn for a 19-17 win.

Big-10 commissioner Kenneth "Tug" Wilson, himself no slouch on the football field, got all excited when he described this Harmon run: "A kickoff return against Penn just might have been the longest run, unofficially, in the history of college football. Taking the ball on the Michigan 17 [Harmon] ripped down the right side of the field where he was hemmed in by three Penn tacklers. He spun out of their clutches, reversed his field all the way to the opposite side and raced down to the Penn 20 only to be pinched in by two more desperate Quaker defenders. Again he reversed his field to the original sideline, tore loose from another clutching Quaker and crossed the goal standing up. It was estimated later that he had gone close to 175 yards, around, through, between and over Red and Blue jerseys."

But losses to Illinois on a trick "sleeper" play by Coach Bob Zuppke, and a bad day against the Minnesota Gophers, 20-7, kept Michigan out of the conference crown race. Then, a great win over Ohio State, the eventual champ, on a fake kick by Harmon and a touchdown sprint by Freddie Trosko thrilled defeat-weary Wolverine fans, who could hardly wait for the following season. Harmon had rushed for 884 yards, passed for 488, and led the nation in scoring with 102 points. He became the first Wolverine halfback since the late-lamented Kipke to be named an All-American.

Those were heady days in the Michigan locker room. Sportswriters and cameramen followed Harmon everywhere he went on campus or during practice. The team was bombarded with newspaper headlines trumpeting things like, "Harmon Greater Than Grange" and "Harmon a One-Man Team." Here Forrest Evashevski proved his maturity and natural leadership qualities by keeping morale and pride high for the rest of the very necessary Wolverine team. He and the other Michigan players delighted in taking their beloved star down a notch or two.

As Harmon would enter the locker room, one of them would shout, "Here comes the team, men. We can practice now!" Once Evy circulated through the locker room loudly trying to recruit new members for an "I-Block-For-Tom-Harmon-Club".

Harmon's 21st birthday, during a game with the California Bears in 1940, was celebrated in high style. The Wolverines had made the nation's first football road trip by air, on three chartered United Airlines

Below: *Coach H.O. "Fritz" Crisler with members of his crack 1940 Wolverine football team (from left to right): Forrest Evashevski, Bob Westfall, Tom Harmon and Freddie Trosko.*

DC-3s. A crowd of 54,000 in Berkeley turned out to watch the talented Michigan team, and of course their star. As the kickoff approached, Evy had a word with the team, out of Harmon's hearing. "This is Tom's 21st birthday," he told them. "Let's give him a present by everybody knocking somebody down!"

He wanted to start the game off with a bang. Pulling Tom aside, Evy whispered to his friend and roommate, "If you get the kickoff, run like a thief and we'll knock a lot of guys down for you."

The kickoff was a boomer, backing Tom Harmon up to the five-yard line. Cutting slightly as Evashevski delivered a crunching block, Harmon scampered 95 yards for his birthday touchdown. He followed it up with a 70-yard punt return for another score, and was preparing to taste the California end zone again, from his own 14, when a crazed Bear fan shook loose from the stands and darting out on the field, dove for Harmon's legs. Luckily, he missed, and Harmon had his third touchdown in a 41-0 pasting.

The rest of that 1940 season went much the same way, with Harmon racking up points left and right in wins over MSU (21-14), Harvard (26-0), Illinois and Pennsylvania. However, the Minnesota Gophers loomed, unbeaten and untied, their domi-

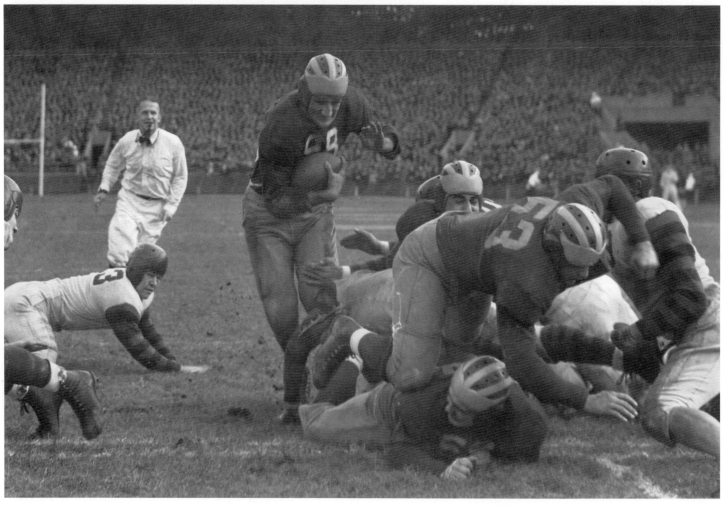

nance of the Wolverines a brick wall to Michigan's title hopes.

On a storm-soaked Saturday the Wolverines drove inside the Minnesota ten three times, only to be thwarted by the enormous Minnesota linemen. The only Michigan touchdown came on a fumble recovery by Harmon and a shovel pass to Evy for the score. Unfortunately, Harmon's extra-point attempt just missed, and the Gophers made a 7-6 advantage hold up.

On the train trip back, gloom settled in. A third straight loss to Minnesota was hard to swallow with Northwestern and Ohio State still left to play. The Wolverine players also wondered how their fans would react. When they got off the train in Ann Arbor, however, a sight met their eyes that Evashevski would never forget. Fans by the hundreds were waiting to meet them. Later he eloquently described the scene: "They had a portable mike, had members of the team say a word, then hoisted us bodily on to a hay rack, and the freshmen pulled us up the long hill to campus. When they all broke into 'The Victors,' it hit a crescendo I couldn't believe. Life had a new meaning."

After a comeback win over Northwestern, the Michigan squad had the spring back in its step as they prepared to face Ohio State in Columbus. Harmon had saved the greatest game in his career for that day.

More than 75,000 fans had packed the place to see if Harmon could break Red Grange's career touchdown record of 31. Harmon's record stood at 30 as the game began, and he quickly tied the mark with an eight-yard scamper. After setting up two more Michigan scores in the first half, Harmon resumed his march to destiny with a run starting at the Ohio 18 – a tearing, slashing run past grasping Buckeye defenders into the end zone for the score, and

the record. A garnish on the day was provided in the final period with a third Harmon touchdown on a pass interception. In the final 15 seconds of the game, as Crisler sat his star down in respect of Ohio State, the stadium exploded with the Buckeye fans' ovation for Harmon – one of the very few times an opposing player has been granted such an honor in Columbus.

With a touchdown total of 33 for his Michigan career, Harmon had also gained 2,338 yards rushing on 398 carries and had completed 101 of 233 passes for another 1,359 yards and 16 TDs. He scored 237 points himself, 33 points-after and two field goals. His scoring places him third on the all-time Michigan record.

Honors showered down upon him. The Heisman Trophy, a second All-America selection, and the Associated Press outstanding male athlete award were all his. But Harmon never experienced so much as a conference title, much less the national championship. If it bothered him, he never let it show. "I am sure that hundreds of football players have enjoyed the experience of wearing the Maize and Blue," he said years later. "But none has enjoyed it more, or appreciated it more, than this very lucky Irishman."

World War II was approaching. Harmon, Evashevski and their merry band left Michigan and some went off to war. But they would remember their days in Ann Arbor.

With service duties again decimating the ranks of players available to him, Crisler had the unwelcome task of putting together a passable Wolverine team in the next few years. In 1941 they did fairly well, going 6-1-1 and losing only to unbeaten national champion Minnesota under outstanding coach Bernie Bierman. Wolverine fullback Bob Westfall ran for 688 yards that year,

Opposite top: *Tom Harmon scampers 19 yards for a touchdown in Ann Arbor during Michigan's 14-0 victory over Penn on October 26, 1940.*

Opposite bottom: *Tom Harmon tallies another touchdown against Penn, at Franklin Field in 1939.*

Above: *A packed grandstand in Ann Arbor watches as Francis Reagan takes the ball upfield against Michigan on October 26, 1940.*

Top: *Tom Harmon (far left) makes a long gain against hated Illinois in Michigan's 28-0 victory in Ann Arbor, October 19, 1940. This grudge match settled the score after the Illini took Michigan out of the conference race the previous year.*

Above: *Fritz Crisler, Michigan's calm and cerebral head coach in the 1940s.*

Opposite: *Bob Chappuis is upended by Lynn Chadnois of Michigan State after receiving a pass from Bump Elliott for a first down, November 9, 1946.*

and made All-American.

In 1942 another Wistert brother, Albert, played tackle, joining guard Julius Franks in a 7-3 season. Wistert and Franks anchored a Michigan line known as the "Seven Oak Posts," and they were key to a great 32-20 win over Notre Dame and crack quarterback Angelo Bertelli that year. Crisler had called an unprecedented indoor practice and assistant coach Bennie Oosterbaan helped teach them some new defensive techniques to use against the Irish — among them the "Red Dog," forerunner to the modern blitz.

The 1943 season, featuring a melting pot of displaced military trainees and regular players, gave Crisler an 8-1 mark and Michigan's first conference championship in 10 years. Among the stars were fullback Bill Daley from Minnesota, Elroy "Crazy Legs" Hirsch from Wisconsin, and his teammate Jack Wink. All-Americans included Daley and defensive stalwart Mervin Pregulman at tackle, both of whom left for the service after only six games.

The seasons of 1944 and 1945 saw Crisler making do mainly with freshmen. He made some experiments that unwittingly changed college football. In a game against a much more experienced Army team, Crisler divided his youngsters between those who were talented defensively, and those who were to be on the passing and kicking side. He lifted eyebrows on the other side of the field by bringing out fresh players with every change in possession. Unwittingly, Crisler had stumbled onto platooning – and the trend would grow quickly throughout the nation.

By the start of the 1946 season the manpower came flooding back to college campuses, and Crisler had 125 varsity candidates come out for Wolverine football. Among them were halfback Bob Chappuis, a veteran of 22 European bombing missions, and wingback Chalmers "Bump" Elliott. He had been a member of Purdue's undefeated 1943 team, and brother Pete had been Crisler's starting quarterback the previous season.

This talented team went 6-2-1 that year, losing only to Army and Illinois. Crisler found he had to help pump some players up and rein in others; with a combination of youth and returning servicemen, the team was still finding itself. However, 26-year-old Elmer Madar was selected an All-American after the season, and Bob Chappuis broke Otto Graham's Big-10 season offense record with a 1,038-yard total.

Before the 1947 season began, Wolverine captain Bruce Hilkene had promised Detroit alumni that this was Michigan's year for the Rose Bowl. And as the Wolverines charged into their season, winning game after game with Howard Yerges at quarterback, fan excitement mounted. MSU, Stanford, Pitt and Northwestern fell before the "dream backfield" of Elliott, Yerges, Jack Weisenburger at fullback, and Chappuis at tailback. Crisler, a little superstitious, forbade his players even to say the words "Rose Bowl."

Not even the intimidating Gophers could stunt this team. Michigan beat them 13-6 with a highlight film 40-yard pass from Chappuis to Elliott.

Illinois, Indiana and Wisconsin were next to fall before the Wolverine attack. The Wisconsin game saw the squad rack up 40 unanswered points, and end Dick Rifenburg, the team cut-up, asked his team-

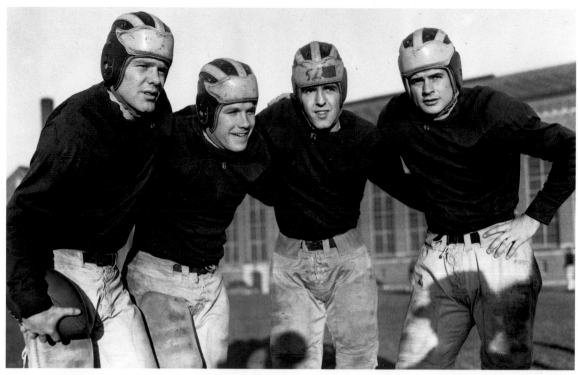

Right: *Michigan's "dream backfield" for the Rose Bowl against USC New Year's Day, 1948. Left to right: Chalmers "Bump" Elliott, right halfback; Howard Yerges, quarterback; Jack Weisenburger, fullback; and Bob Chappuis, left halfback.*

Right: *Coach Bennie Oosterbaan with Wolverine Captain Dominick Tomasi in 1948.*

mates in the huddle, "Do you think it's okay now to mention R-O-S-E B-O-W-L?"

It was. Only the Buckeyes stood between them and a date in Pasadena, and Michigan coasted to an easy 21-0 win. Next stop, California, to face USC.

As the Santa Fe Super Chief headed west, Crisler must have worried about his team's possible overconfidence. He need not have. A stunned New Year's Day crowd watched as fullback Weisenburger stormed for three TDs, Chappuis passed to Elliott for another, and Yerges and Hank Fonde scored in turn for a 49-0 holocaust.

Michigan had produced a Bowl record 491 yards of offense, and had exactly duplicated the 49-0 score achieved by Yost's long-ago squad. The Wolverines were voted national champions, with a season total of 1,625 yards of offense.

Both Chappuis and Elliott made All-American; they had been part of a backfield Crisler described as "the greatest group of ball-handlers I ever saw."

The national crown made it easier for Crisler to announce his retirement from coaching, but his decision still disappointed his many fans. Like Yost before him, Crisler wanted to devote his energies to running Michigan athletics. And there was more to it. As he later recalled, "It was only a matter of time before the college would seek the man, instead of the man seeking the college. And, personally, I would never to be able to recruit." He would leave that to those who came later.

Loyal assistant Bennie Oosterbaan had earned his chance at the helm. Crisler called him, "the one man who could retain our single wing, and the finest football mind I know." It would have been difficult to convince fans and alumni, but Michigan's years of greatest fame still lay ahead.

During the 1948 season Oosterbaan managed to preserve the single-wing attack. Although the "dream backfield" had graduated, he had the aerial duo of QB Pete Elliott and end Rifenburg. Alvin Wistert, the third brother to wear number 11 for Michigan, anchored a crack line at age 32, following several years of service in the Marines.

It was a good season indeed, with the Wolverines going 9-0 again, repeating as national champions. Only the Rose Bowl non-repeat rule, barring consecutive appearances, kept Michigan from traveling to Pasadena again.

Not only did Pete Elliott, Rifenburg and Wistert make All-America teams, but Oosterbaan earned Coach of the Year honors. Never before had different coaches at the same university been given this honor in successive seasons.

Oosterbaan's 1949 squad had lost a lot of experience and savvy to graduation, but still posted a 6-2-1 mark. The loss to undefeated Army, 21-7, brought the Wolverines' 25-game win streak to an end, but Michigan consoled itself with a share of the Big-10 title – its third consecutive conference championship. Backfield stalwart Chuck Ortmann led the conference in total offense, and Alvin Wistert was named an All-American once again – joined by fellow tackle Allen Wahl.

In 1950 the Michigan Wolverines began a new decade by winning a fourth straight conference title, although the team was not as strong overall as in previous championship years. Wahl repeated as All-American, but the highlight of the year was the infamous Ohio State – Michigan "Blizzard Bowl." The two squads slugged it out in a blinding snowstorm and punting decided the contest, as visibility dropped to near zero in the second half. The Wolverines pulled it out, 9-3, to earn their third Rose Bowl appearance.

They topped off the season, and rang in the new year, with a 14-6 victory over the favored California Bears, coached by Lynn "Pappy" Waldorf. The game featured two touchdowns from Don Dufek and the passing of Chuck Ortmann for 146 yards.

But the decade that had started so well would prove to be the most difficult in the history of the University of Michigan.

5. Times of Struggle 1951-1968

As Fritz Crisler had foreseen, by the 1950s the schools were seeking the athletes. After all, there are only so many outstanding high school prospects in a given year, and these youngsters now had a wide choice of schools. Good programs abounded in the Big-10, yes, but there were also the Pacific 10, Southeast, Big-8 and Southwestern conferences to consider.

It may also have been, simply, that the rest of the country had caught up to Michigan. Televised games and sophisticated scouting gave opponents and other interested teams instant access to any coaching or field innovation Michigan pioneered. As a perennial power, they provided the motivation often needed by inferior teams to pull an upset.

Lastly, Michigan coaches were unaccustomed to the type of effort that was now required to entice the best players in the country to come to Ann Arbor. College football had exploded all over the country, and skilled recruitment was now essential in staying competitive. Honest college recruiting proved ineffective, and Bennie Oosterbaan's last eight years as head coach produced a record of 42-28-2 from 1951 to 1958. It would have been a respectable mark at many schools, but not for the University of Michigan.

Not that Wolverine teams did not produce All-Americans here and there. End Lowell Perry was named All-American in 1951, and in 1954 tackle Art Walker was so honored. End Ron Kramer, who was also a part of the 1954 squad, spearheaded the 1955 team as well – one which posted a 7-2 record. Kramer, an exceptional athlete, made All-America in both 1955 and 1956.

Unfortunately, this very period was producing spectacular teams in Columbus, as coach Wayne Woodrow "Woody" Hayes was fielding Buckeye teams featuring stars like slashing runner Howard "Hopalong" Cassady. With Buckeye football in its Golden

Below: *Michigan's coaching staff in 1953, led by Bennie Oosterbaan on the far left.*

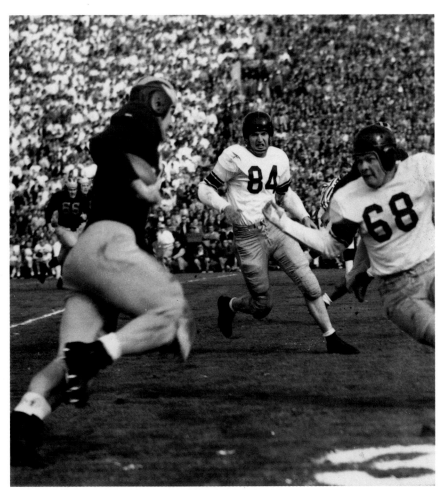

Era, the Wolverines seemed destined to be also-rans, and Hayes' name became a hated one in Ann Arbor.

By the end of the 1958 season, with a 2-6-1 record and only the All-America selection of halfback Jim Pace to cheer about, the grumbling from alumni and fans grew louder. Oosterbaan began to talk of retirement, and the rumor was that 30-year-old Pete Elliott, now coaching Nebraska, would be named to replace him. Instead, it was Bump Elliott who came to the rescue. He was hired away from Iowa, where Forrest Evashevski was now installed as head coach.

Bennie Oosterbaan's later years had been unlucky, with injuries and a drain of player talent. But his gentle wisdom, caring attitude and insistence on fair play and honesty had made him beloved among his players. As both a Wolverine player and coach, Oosterbaan had brought honor to his university, and his 1958 squad carried him off the field on their shoulders after his last game. He stayed on as supervisor of alumni and public relations.

Chalmers "Bump" Elliott became the Big-10's youngest coach at the beginning of the 1959 season. In taking the reins, he pulled no punches with alumni and sportswriters in assessing Michigan's distance from respectability. "It will take three to five years to rebuild and win a champion-

Above left: *Michigan fullback Don Dufek rips off some yardage against California in the 1951 Rose Bowl game, which Michigan won 14-6.*

Above: *Great All-American end Ron Kramer, who led Michigan's teams in 1954-56, leaps to snare a 17-yard Jimmy Maddock pass in 1955.*

Left: *Chalmers "Bump" Elliott, Michigan's head football coach from 1959 to 1968. Later he would be Iowa's longtime Athletic Director.*

Above: *All-American quarterback Bob Timberlake led Michigan to its Big-10 Championship in 1964.*

Opposite top: *Michigan halfback Carl Ward is tripped up after a short gainer against Michigan State in the 1965 game in Ann Arbor.*

Opposite bottom: *Mel Anthony on his way to an 84-yard touchdown run against Oregon State in the 1965 Rose Bowl, which Michigan won 34-7. Tom Mack keeps a Beaver defender at bay.*

ship," he told them. Indeed, it wasn't until 1964 that the formula came together, but it was well worth the wait.

This is the kind of luck Elliott and the Wolverines experienced in the early 1960s. Promising end Bill Freehan left the squad to sign a contract to pitch for the Detroit Tigers. Two other promising talents, center Joe Sligay and tackle Phil Garrison, were killed in accidents. At the end of the 1962 season, Elliott's Michigan squad found itself dead last in the Big-10 standings – the first time that had happened since 1936.

But by the end of the 1963 season, Elliott thought he could sense the beginnings of a change. He had a smart, quick QB in Bob Timberlake, who had led the Big-10 in rushing. Timberlake could pass and place kick almost as well as run. Two sophomores in the backfield, Carl Ward and Jim Detwiler, showed promise. And Mel Anthony was a classic fullback. Linebackers, tackles and ends were solid.

However, the season began with some special people missing from the Wolverine family. One of them was equipment manager Henry Hatch. For 43 years he had sewn, mended, repaired and invented equipment, all the while treating each player, from star to scrub, like a father. Henry Hatch had died. Not long after, Ralph Aigler passed away – a longtime Wolverine supporter, instrumental in getting Michigan back into the conference. The retirement of Fielding Yost in 1941 had

started this slow but inevitable fading away of the human links to the "old days."

So Elliott was determined to start some "new days" of his own. Early in the 1964 season the squad began to show its promise, shutting Navy out with 148 combined yards for Detwiler and Ward. Middie QB Roger Staubach, nursing an injured heel, wasn't a factor in the 21-0 Michigan win.

The third game of the season was a battle with MSU, one that many observers later called the key to the season. Rick Sygar caught a Timberlake pass in the fourth quarter for a touchdown, then tossed his own 31-yard pass to John Henderson to clinch a 17-0 win. The victory inched Michigan up to fifth place in the polls, and fans began to believe in the team's ability to control its own destiny.

There was no time to celebrate, however, as the following week the Purdue "Spoilermakers" managed to steal a 21-20 upset on three Michigan fumbles.

Next was a typical hard-fought victory over Minnesota which featured the Wolverines toying with a 19-point lead and almost blowing it before holding off the Gophers 19-12. It was a sweet win – the first one over Minnesota in five long years for Elliott.

Northwestern and Illinois fell before the newly-confident squad, 35-0 and 21-6 respectively. A 34-20 win over Iowa set up the game everyone had waited for: Michigan against nemesis OSU, with the Big-10 Crown and a Rose Bowl trip on the line.

A Friday night pep rally had Wolverine fans in a frenzy, and thousands made the trip to Columbus. "Go, go, go!" they were chanting as the Wolverines took the field.

"I think we're ready to play a game," commented Elliott.

The first half was pure, down-and-dirty, Big-10 football as both teams battled each other and the gusty 18-mph wind.

Finally, late in the second half, Ohio State's normally sure-handed Bo Rein fumbled a punt return and Henderson scooped up the ball on OSU's 20. Michigan's custom-made "trailer play" had Ben Farabee sprint from end, trailed by Detwiler, then cut over the middle to draw defenders and leave Detwiler clear. He gathered in a perfectly placed Timberlake pass on the four, skipping over the goal. Timberlake's extra point upped the score to 7-0; later a field goal locked in a 10-0 win and the crown – at last!

After the elated Wolverines carried Bump Elliott off the field on their shoulders, he told reporters, "This is my happiest moment in football."

That proved a premature statement on the coach's part. The Rose Bowl game with Oregon State demonstrated that his Michi-

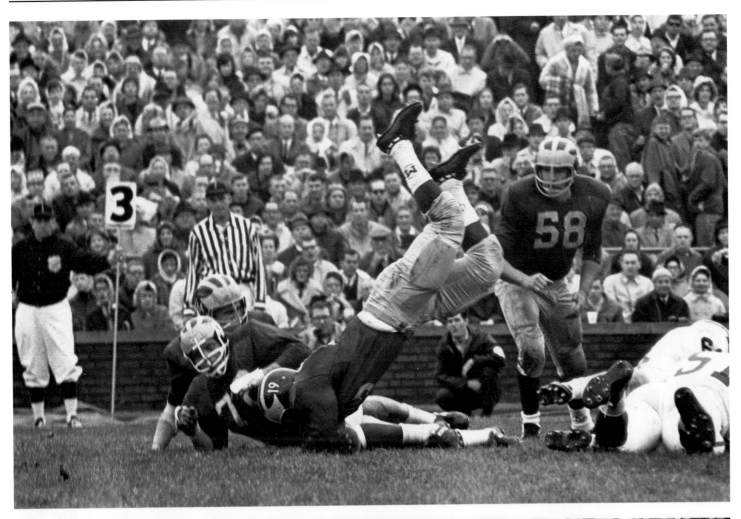

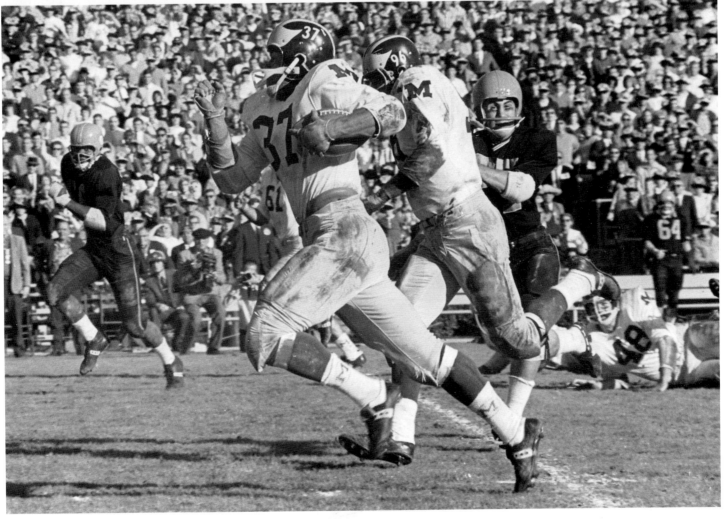

Right: *All-American tackle Bill Yearby inspired terror in 1964.*

gan squad had the killer instinct. In front of more than 100,000 fans they whipped the outmanned Ducks 34-7, as Mel Anthony set a Rose Bowl record with an 87-yard touchdown and scored twice more. When it was over, his players laid the game ball in Elliott's lap.

Timberlake and tackle Bill Yearby made the All-America list, and Anthony took home Rose Bowl MVP honors. Unfortunately for Elliott, however, the roof seemed to fall in the following season. The Wolverines, favored to repeat as Big-10 cham-

pions, managed only a 4-6 season.

Although Yearby repeated as an All-American in 1965, followed by backs Rick Volk and John Clancy in 1966, Michigan could not pull together success as a team. The 1966 and 1967 seasons are best forgotten, as the squad produced records of 6-4 and 4-6 respectively.

In 1968 brilliant junior halfback Ron Johnson gave the fans a reason to leap to their feet. The year before he had become the first Michigan runner to break 1,000 yards and was voted MVP by his team-

Left: *Ron Johnson carries the ball against Purdue during the 1968 season in which he broke Tom Harmon's career rushing record.*

mates. This year he was also team captain – the very first black player so honored at Michigan – and seemed intent upon earning their accolades.

Not even a dislocated thumb, suffered just before the opening of his senior season, could deter him. Asked if the injury would bother him, Johnson replied, "I'll just have to carry the ball in the other hand."

He paced the Wolverines to a eight-game win rampage before they took on Wisconsin and OSU.

Against the Badgers, the durable back ripped off runs of 35, 67 and 60 yards for scores. When Elliott finally sat his star down after his fifth touchdown, he received a Michigan Stadium ovation. The 34-9 rout also marked Johnson's breaking of Tom Harmon's career rushing record, and a college record-breaking 347 yards from scrimmage as a runner.

The favored Buckeyes, however, completed their campaign for the national championship by beating Michigan 50-14. Woody Hayes' squad had done it again, and the following year the Wolverines would

Above: *Team captains for Michigan and Ohio State shake hands prior to the infamous 1968 ground war, in which Ohio State Coach Woody Hayes ran up the score against Michigan, 50-14. Michigan got its revenge the following year.*

wear practice jerseys emblazoned with the number "50."

But for now it was time to look back on a great season, and to toast Johnson. In addition to All-America honors, the modest back was named MVP by both his Michigan teammates and the *Chicago Tribune*. Last came this tribute from his coach: "He was the best football player and best captain I had during my coaching career."

Weeks after the season ended, Elliott announced that his career had come to a close. He had accepted the position of assistant athletic director to Fritz Crisler's successor, Don Canham. Eventually he would take over as athletic director at Iowa, where he has been ever since.

Elliott was respected and popular with fans and alumni. They hated to see him go, but they had no way of knowing that his replacement – Glenn E. "Bo" Schembechler – would be the most famous Wolverine coach in history.

"At first, they wanted bigger names than me," Schembechler recalled in his book, *Bo*. "But at the time the program was down, and men like Joe Paterno, who they coveted, were not really interested. Eventually, they got around to me. I flew up for an interview on a Sunday, checked into a hotel under an assumed name, met all day

with Don Canham, the Athletic Director, then flew back home.

"Sure enough, I was offered the job. I was in the office of my friend Joe Hayden when I officially accepted. I hung up and said, 'Well, Joe, that's it. I'm going to Ann Arbor. Back to the Big-10.'

'Great. How much are they paying you?' I looked at him and laughed. 'I have no idea,' I said."

"They don't call you every day of the week and talk to you about the Michigan job," he later told reporters. "I hoped at the time Bump didn't notice the excitement in my voice."

Bo Schembechler from Barberton, Ohio, who had once spied on a Wolverine practice as a kid on a family vacation, was now their head coach. He brought with him a rich coaching background: assistant and good friend of Woody Hayes at OSU, then on to "cradle of coaches" Miami of Ohio as head coach.

Schembechler would be the first Wolverine coach to be faced with the true torrent of modern football media, and he understood how to cope with these and other modern pressures. In an era when many middle-aged white football coaches were having trouble relating to, and motivating, their black players, Bo knew how to treat every man in the clubhouse the same – "like dogs," as he used to say.

The University of Michigan in 1969 was a highly academic, politically active place where football, once part of the lifeblood of the campus, did not seem relevant to many students. Facilities were looking a little shabby and out-of-date. Bo later described his first tour of inspection of the football complex – much of which had not changed since Yost's day: "Football was not the number one priority. One look at the facilities told you that. In the beginning, believe it or not, we coaches slept in the clubhouse on the golf course. We walked across the greens to get to work. I remember entering our dressing room at Yost Field House and seeing nothing but a wooden two-by-four, bolted to the wall, with a couple of nails sticking out. The nails were our lockers.

'Men,' I said, seeing the looks on my coaches' faces, 'we are going to make a few changes here.'"

Bo got to work. He nailed up a sign on the locker room door that read, "Those Who Stay Will Be Champions." It would be his unofficial slogan at Michigan.

Meanwhile, Don Canham, who had given Schembechler his word that he had five years to turn the Michigan football program around, was busy using some modern marketing techniques to fill up the too-often-empty seats of Michigan Stadium. But he knew nothing would work better than a winning team.

Above: *Michigan's head football coach Glenn "Bo" Schembechler replaced Bump Elliott at the beginning of the 1969 season, and led Michigan to a surprising 24-12 victory over previously unbeaten Ohio State. The season cost him his first heart attack.*

Left: *Michigan Stadium – minus 106,000 screaming fans!*

6. Champions of the West 1969-present

Coach Bo Schembechler's first season produced an 8-3 mark and his first Big-10 title. Once his talented players got used to the new coach's methods, they produced for him in abundance.

Junior quarterback Don Moorhead ran and passed for 1,886 yards of total offense, aided by Jim Mandich at tight end, who caught 50 of his passes for 676 yards.

To top off Bo's very first season at the helm, the Wolverines had a nasty surprise ready for his old mentor – now his arch-foe – Woody Hayes. As fate would have it, visiting Ohio State stood in Bo's way of a Rose Bowl. Schembechler later described the manic halftime scene in the locker room as the Wolverines led 24-12: "Ohio State was stunned. With just over a minute left in the half, we were up 24-12. No other team had scored more than 21 points on the Buckeyes *all year* – and here we had 24 *by halftime*! You absolutely could not hear yourself think! We left the field to an ovation that was still ringing in our ears when we poured into the locker room.

"And what a scene *that* was. Players roaring. Coaches screaming. Jim Young, our defensive coordinator, who is normally a fairly reserved guy, stood in front of the blackboard and began pounding it over and over. 'They . . . will . . . not . . . score . . . again! Gentlemen, I promise you they . . . WILL (pound) NOT (pound) SCORE (pound) AGAIN!'"

In a defensive masterpiece the second half, the Wolverines in fact did not allow OSU to score and pulled off a stunning upset, 24-12, before more than 105,000 fans. It is still remembered by many fans and alumni as the day football mania was reborn in Ann Arbor, Michigan.

"The rest, I must admit, is a blur," recalled Schembechler. "The field was mobbed. Tom Curtis, my senior safety, would later tell me that in the final minute, he turned and saw a high school buddy standing next to him on the sidelines. How he got there, I have no idea. I guess even the security guards were celebrating. Fans were everywhere. The goalposts were

Right: *Rival coaches and former colleagues Bo Schembechler and Woody Hayes shake hands prior to the Ohio State-Michigan game. The "Ten-Year War" was already underway.*

broken down. The band was blasting, 'California, Here We Come.' I was lost in a sea of arms, legs and helmets. I was bouncing on players' shoulders. Our locker room was a mass assembly of players, fans and reporters. They were calling it the 'upset of the decade'. All that night, people came by my house, stangers, people I had never met, just to say what a great win it had been. We watched the sun rise, too excited to sleep."

For Hayes, it was the one loss he never got over. At a dinner years later, he recalled how great that Buckeye team had been, and how sure he had been that they would beat the Wolverines. Then, searching out Schembechler in the crowd, he glared down at him and yelled, "Goddamn you, Bo! You will *never* win a bigger game than that one!"

Meanwhile, fan interest and participation were undergoing a revival of sorts from the hippie decade just completed. Michigan fans, boosters and band members had often taken their cues from the head football coach himself. Wolverine fans under Fielding Yost had mirrored the cocky, boastful style of the confident coach, especially when it came to taunting Michigan's rivals. During a game with Ohio State in 1902, Michigan fans adapted a Buckeye cheer to

their own uses, and chanted throughout the game:

> What will we do?
> What will we do?
> We'll rub it into OSU,
> That's what we'll do!

By the way, the Wolverine players backed up the chant by pasting Ohio State 86-0 for their easiest Buckeye win ever.

With Bo Schembechler as coach, fans and boosters again felt justified in swaggering a bit. Colorful players of the seventies also contributed to the general air of confidence. Once before an Ohio State game, All-American tight end and free spirit Jim Mandich told a manic pep rally crowd, "We're gonna kick – – – and take names!"

Ann Arbor residents took to the Schembechlers immediately, although that sometimes presented problems of its own. Here's how the coach describes it in his book, *Bo*: "Millie and I have lived in the same house in Ann Arbor since 1969, and just about everybody knows where it is. Kids will ring the bell and ask for autographs. That's OK. It's when they take my license plates that I get a little annoyed. One morning I came out and both the plates were taken off my

Above: *Everybody needs someone to hate. Wolverine fans express their fondness for the OSU coach.*

car. They're on some frat house wall, I bet.

"Sometimes, in the middle of the night, a car will roll by and a student will scream, 'Hey, Bo, wake up!' And if we leave a Michigan flag outside, like we used to on game day, forget it. Someone takes off with it. We've been given maize-and-blue Christmas ornaments . . . and toilet paper. Now and then, if people know Millie is out of town, I'll come home to find a couple frozen steaks on the front step with a note: 'Bo – figured you could use some dinner. . . .'"

The marching band and the cheerleaders have been an important part of Michigan lore. Until relatively recently, both the Wolverine marching band and the cheerleading squad were all-male bastions. Women have only gained unlimited access to athletic facilities and field houses in the last decade.

Currently the Wolverine cheerleaders feature 10 men and 10 women students, chosen on the basis of talent tryouts. Although a coed squad was finally established for the 1984-85 season, the group was not officially recognized by the university until 1986. Various traditional "pom squads" made up of female students have been a part of the athletic scene throughout the 1980s. The Wolverine cheerleaders perform at all home games, travel with the team to two away contests, and of course ac-

company the players to postseason bowl games.

The marching band, established in 1896 as an informal group of musically talented fans who disdained uniforms, now numbers some 320 musicians – although "only" 225 members actually march during games. Partially because of its existence as an ROTC organization until the late 1940s, the marching band was all-male by tradition until 1972, and it was not until 1973 that the first women actually played in the band. However, female band members now account for 43 percent of the group.

Halftime programs between Ohio State and Michigan have become band extravaganzas, as both marching bands execute their trademark formations, Wolverine bands form the letter M, and the Ohio State band performs its script Ohio State, with one lucky player having the honor of dotting the "i" in Ohio.

Other Wolverine marching band traditions include the singing of the University of Michigan alma mater in the tunnel as the band awaits its march onto the field. It's done not as a performance, but strictly for members' ears.

Michigan's fight song, "The Victors," is among the most famous in the country. The Wolverine marching band actually performs the entire tune "as written" only in

Above right: *It is a Michigan tradition for the drum major to touch his tassle to the ground during the pre-game ceremonies.*

Far right: *Only recently has Michigan permitted female cheerleaders.*

Right: *An all-male bastion until the past decade, Michigan cheerleaders have always displayed their own brand of humor.*

Right: *The University of Michigan Marching Band – a proud tradition dating back to ROTC roots.*

Above left: *Coach Bo Schembechler and his son "Schemy" after the Rose Bowl victory over Washington in 1981.*

Above: *The Michigan team takes the field, and leaps to touch the "Go Blue" sign for luck.*

Far left: *The Michigan drum major on the field with the band at halftime.*

Left: *Jubilant Wolverines congratulate each other after a rousing touchdown.*

Bottom: *Michigan's 1977 team celebrates a victory over Ohio State – always the highlight of the season.*

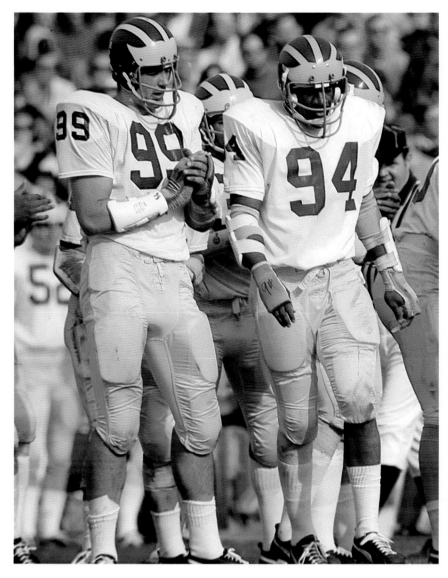

concert and during events like the Rose Parade. Like Notre Dame's Victory March, many football fans have heard the refrain and can hum it, even if they don't know the words. And, of course, for Michigan alumni the song brings back a storehouse of treasured memories. "When you hear it in Michigan Stadium, played by the full band, it's like the national anthem," one alumnus has commented.

Yes, Michigan was back as Bo Schembechler's first season neared completion. But the challenges of the season had taken a toll on the new coach. Just before the Michigan players were to play USC in the 1970 Rose Bowl, they were told that Schembechler had suffered a mild heart attack and been taken to a Pasadena hospital. As some of his players walked over to a nearby chapel, others pondered the upcoming game. Recalled defensive back Frank Gusich, "I thought, we'll kick the hell out of them. But it wasn't what I felt. I felt down, cold, like the fire had gone out."

The glamour had gone out of the game for the team, coaches, officials and writers, and the Wolverines went down to a 10-3 defeat at the hands of the USC Trojans, in an un-

spectacular and uninspired game.

All throughout spring practice players and fellow coaches wondered whether Schembechler could come back. They had trouble convincing some newly-recruited talent that Coach of the Year Bo would indeed return to Michigan. Finally, the slimmed-down Schembechler took up the reins again, and the results were quite heartening.

The 1970 Wolverines featured returning All-Americans Jim Mandich and safety Tom Curtis, plus co-captains Don Moorhead and middle guard Henry Hill. Backs Glenn Doughty and Billy Taylor were ready, and very few sophomores on the team that year expected to start. The Wolverines under Schembechler were back to a deep bench.

By the Michigan State game, the Wolverines were looking tough again, and a Stadium crowd of 103,508 watched as Taylor became the first Michigan player since Bob Chappuis to score three touchdowns on the Spartans. Doughty, playing wingback, scored another. Taylor gained 151 yards the following week as the Wolverines knocked off Minnesota. A 29-15 win against Wiscon-

Opposite: *Co-captain Don Moorhead fades back to pass during the Ohio State game in 1970. Michigan lost 20-9.*

Above left: *Linemen create a formidable wall in front of crack halfback Billy Taylor during the 1971 Purdue game.*

Above: *Halfback Glenn Doughty runs his pattern during the Ohio State game in 1971.*

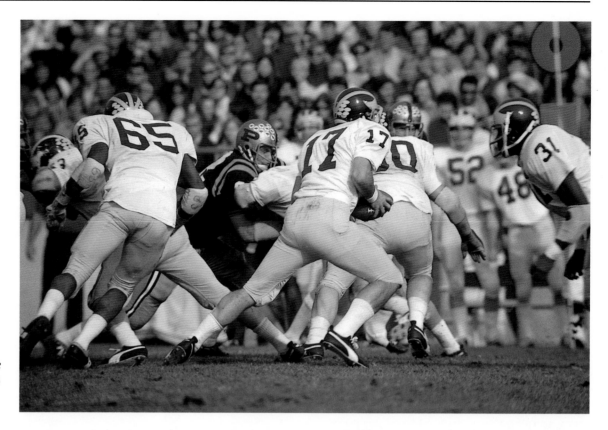

sin came next, before the Wolverine offense racked up 97 points in two games against Illinois and Iowa in successive shutouts.

But the Ohio State game loomed, and the fans knew Schembechler had his heart set on this one. OSU, however, had revenge on its side. Woody Hayes had a rug emblazoned with the previous year's score (24-12) placed at the entrance to the Buckeye locker room where each player had to look at it every day, and his troops, including Jack Tatum, Rex Kern and John Brockington, were ready. It was the beginning of the Hayes-Schembechler battle football fans later named The Ten-Year War. This day, however, belonged to the Buckeyes in a 20-9 win for a trip to California. They were upset in the Rose Bowl by Stanford, 27-17 – but the rivalry with Michigan, dampened during the 1950s and 1960s, was in full flower once again.

And so it went through the 1970s. Schembechler's personal Golden Era lasted from 1971 to 1974, during which he posted four consecutive Big-10 championships, three shared and one which belonged to them alone. All over again, other Big-10 fans learned to groan at the maize-and-blue wave rolling over them year after year.

The Wolverines were throwing off All-Americans like sparks off a bonfire: in 1970 the All-Americans had been Marty Huff, Dan Dierdorf and Henry Hill. From the 1971 squad Billy Taylor, Mike Taylor, Reggie McKenzie and safety Tom Darden gained honors. In 1972 defensive halfback Randy Logan and 250-pound tackle Paul Seymour were chosen. In 1973 the unde-

feated Wolverines contributed defensive tackle Dave Gallagher and safety Dave Brown.

But there had been disappointments too. A rainy field for the 1972 Rose Bowl had meant his team was ill-prepared to play Stanford – Bo had even joked that he felt his old chest pains returning. The result of the game, however, was no joke: 13-12 on a fourth-quarter field goal by Rod Garcia. Bo later admitted he had made a mistake in ordering his players to wear long spikes, when the Stanford players were sporting short cleats or turf shoes. "I think we were tired from using the longer cleats by the time the game was over," he recalled later.

But it was a 1973 vote on who would go to the Rose Bowl that Schembechler called one of his biggest disappointments. The "big one" that year with OSU had resulted in a hard-fought tie, in which QB Denny Franklin had received a broken collarbone. A tie for the conference title was the result, and a vote was called on which team to send to Pasadena. Big-10 Commissioner Wayne Duke, perhaps reflecting on the last four Rose Bowl defeats for the Big-10 against the Pac-10, prevailed upon conference athletic directors to send OSU.

Schembechler's fit of rage when he heard the news from a reporter before taping his weekly TV show, is now legendary. As he recalls it, "I was speechless. I walked away from the crowd, went into the studio, and began kicking everything in sight. Trash cans. Chairs. I have never been so angry in my life. . . . I marched out. I was damn near crying. I mean, you don't do things like this, not to those kids who played all year and didn't lose a game. 'You guys don't deserve this . . . ,' I told them the following morning. And I broke down."

He would always remember the slight from the Big-10's brass, and thereafter he and Wayne Duke were rarely invited to the same cocktail parties.

But the Bo Schembechler years at Michigan continued to be very good ones. At the end of the 1974 season, his personal five-year record stood at 48-6-1, and there were few critics in Ann Arbor. In addition to being an inspired coach, Schembechler was a truly tireless recruiter and friend of alumni. To recruit a hot prospect, appear at an alumni dinner, and just talk football with his endless list of friends and admirers, he would put in long hours of hard work.

Bo continued to amass winning seasons into the early 1980s, and even after his mentor-nemesis, Woody Hayes, was forced into retirement by his own uncontrollable temper, the games with Ohio State continued to be the highlight of the year. Bowl games came almost every year: between 1975 and 1986 Bo's Wolverines had garnered six conference titles and trips to many of the "lesser" bowl games as well. Orange, Gator, Sugar and Bluebonnet Bowls kept fan interest high and the recruiting hot, even if the Wolverines never seemed to perform at their best during these postseason showcases.

Take the Rose Bowls, for example.

Above: *Safety Dave Brown looks for an interception in 1974.*

Left: *Michigan tailback Butch Woolfolk (24) runs for a short gain against the Iowa Hawkeyes. The Michigan rushing record set by Woolfolk in the early 1980s was broken by Jamie Morris later in the decade.*

Schembechler has this explanation in his autobiography about why the Big-10 fared so poorly in Pasadena during the late 1970s: "In the seventies, the Michigan-Ohio State game was so big that, to be honest, the Rose Bowl seemed anticlimactic. We were never able to reach the same peak twice. Sure, I wanted to win those early Rose Bowls, but not as much as I wanted to beat Ohio State and Woody. And I think he felt the same way. Woody's record in the Rose Bowl during the Ten-Year War was 1-4. His overall bowl record during that time was 2-6. So he wasn't faring much better than me."

The Rose Bowl bogey was finally laid to rest for Schembechler after the 1980 season. The Wolverines posted a 10-2 mark, winning their last eight games to take Michigan's 30th Big-10 title. Butch Woolfolk had moved the ball 1,042 yards for a Michigan record, and Anthony Carter nabbed 51 passes for 818 yards and 14 touchdowns. This team was special. The Michigan victory over Washington, 23-6, in the 1981 Rose Bowl broke the jinx which Pasadena had seemed to hold over Coach Bo. "We finally won a Rose Bowl," Bo recalled. "I must have sighed for a half hour." The monkey was finally off his back.

Along the way he gained a reputation as a true student of Woody Hayes when it came to throwing headphones, yelling at officials and generally screaming his outrage at anything that wasn't going his way. He describes the pressure of being on the sidelines: "Picture this: you are wearing a headset, and in your ears you can hear all the coaches in the press box, plus all the people on the sidelines who have the same headset. The crowd around you is roaring, so you have to scream to be heard. Your heart is pounding. Your pulse is racing. You are so locked in the strategy of the game that a bomb could go off in your underwear and you wouldn't notice. You can feel when things are going your way. You can see the mistakes you made and wish to hell you hadn't. You're thinking about tendencies and formations and personnel and play-calling and what down it is, and what yard line it is, and which way the wind is blowing, and who's your hot running back, and all the time you're doing this, there's a 25-second clock going tick, tick, tick.

"Now, this is not the place to take aside one of your players and calmly say, 'Tommy, tell me how you are feeling. Is everything OK? Do you think you'll be able to catch this screen pass if we throw it to you?' We are not in a negotiating position here. We are not here to discuss theory. Damn it, man. We're at war out there."

In 1984 Schembechler's Michigan squad went 6-6, his worst season ever. The following year, however, they were back to 10 wins, and in 1986 went 11-2, climaxed by a 26-24 victory over Ohio State to win the conference title. Schembechler's QB that year was Jim Harbaugh, who had guaranteed a win before the game. He has gone on to quarterbacking success with the Chicago Bears. The Rose Bowl that year, however, ended with Arizona State on top, 22-15.

In 1989 Schembechler won another pre-

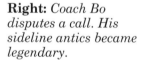

Right: *Coach Bo disputes a call. His sideline antics became legendary.*

Left: *All-American quarterback Jim Harbaugh showing his amazing mobility during the 1986 Ohio State clash.*

Left: *Bryan Carpenter intercepts a Washington pass in the second quarter of the 1981 Rose Bowl. Michigan won the game, 23-6.*

cious Rose Bowl with a 22-14 victory over USC. Many say it was a second victory in Pasadena which enabled him to make a tough decision about his future with the Wolverines.

The list of Schembechler's stars and All-Americans is almost staggering. Quarterbacks included Harbaugh, who became the first Michigan quarterback to throw for 2,000 yards in a season, and Rick Leach, QB of Bo's late-seventies Wolverines who kept winning the conference title but losing the Rose Bowl. All Leach did was total 1,723 and 1,894 yards of total offense in 1977 and 1978 respectively, before going on to a major league baseball career.

Runners Bo had aplenty. There was Gordon Bell in 1974 and 1975, who ran for 1,048 and 1,388 yards respectively. There was Rob Lytle, who ran for 1,469 yards and 16 TDs in 1975 to help the Wolverines lead the nation in total offense, rushing, scoring average and scoring defense. And there was Anthony Carter, whom Bo called, "the best receiver I ever had and the most exciting player I ever coached."

Other All-Americans included Ron Simpkins in 1979, Carter, Ed Muranski and Kurt Becker in 1981, and a repeat selection of Carter in 1982. All-Americans for the 1985 season included Brad Cochran and Mike Hammerstein. Jim Harbaugh com-

Above: *Michigan quarterback Rick Leach hands off to halfback Russell Davis during the 1976 Ohio State game. Michigan won, 22-0.*

Right: *Gordon Bell ran for over 1,000 yards in both the 1974 and 1975 seasons. He would be disappointed this day against OSU in 1974, as Michigan lost 12-10.*

Far right: *Jamie Morris carries the mail during the 1986 Ohio State game. Michigan won.*

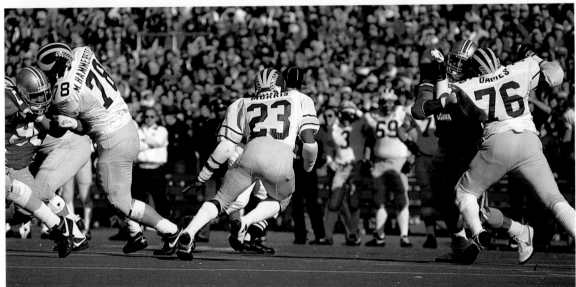

Left: *Three-time All-American Anthony Carter sprints for a score against Notre Dame in 1981. Michigan won, 26-7.*

Below left: *Jamie Morris, shown here in the 1986 Ohio State game, was one of Michigan's all-time leading rushers. Morris holds the Michigan record for most net yards rushing, with 4,393.*

Bottom left: *Mike Gillette boots a field goal during Michigan's victory over Ohio State in 1986. Gillette was one of the greatest place-kickers in Michigan history; he holds career records for most field goals scored (57) and most PATs scored (130).*

Below: *Battle-scarred Rob Lytle helped lead Michigan in total offense nationally, and to a victory in the 1976 Ohio State game.*

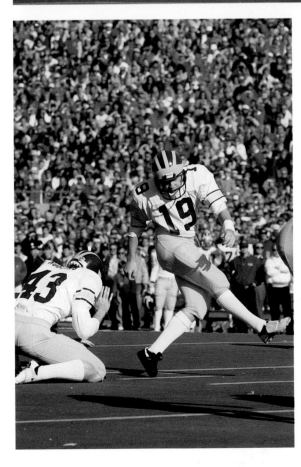

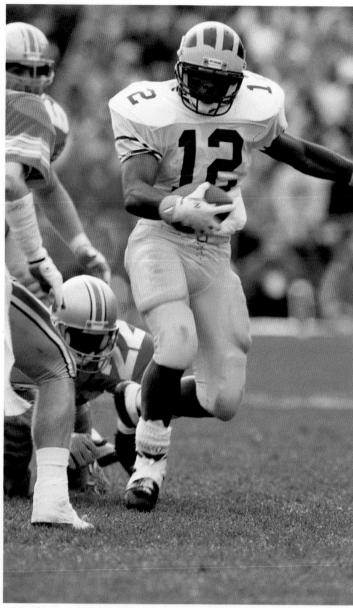

Above: *Elvis Grbac directed Michigan's offense to victory in the 1990 Ohio State game.*

Above right: *Ricky Powers was the sensational tailback who replaced Jon Vaughn in mid-season and went on to propel Michigan to its 16-13 victory over Ohio State, November 1990.*

bined 1986 All-America status with selection as Big-10 MVP.

On New Year's Day of 1990 Bo Schembechler announced he was retiring from coaching Michigan football and his position as Athletic Director to take over the Detroit Tigers baseball team. He left having compiled these astonishing statistics: winning or sharing 13 Big-10 titles in 21 years as coach, going to 17 bowl games including 10 Rose Bowls, and finishing Wolverine teams in the Top Ten 15 times. He's Michigan's winningest coach with 194 victories and 22 All-Americans.

He never won a national title, or coached a Heisman Trophy winner. He will try not to let that bother him, as he has turned over the coaching reins to longtime assistant Gary Moeller.

Moeller has a hard act to follow. His 1990 Wolverines were sound and finished 9-3, after losing a mid-season heartbreaker by one point to Michigan State, in which a Michigan TD was mistakenly ruled invalid. Moeller's 1990 squad then capped the

season by trouncing Mississippi, 35-3, in the 1991 Gator Bowl on New Year's Day. The game was notable not only for the lopsided score, but for the four touchdown passes thrown by Wolverine quarterback Elvis Grbac.

In rolling up a Gator Bowl-record 715 yards of offense and 35 first downs, Moeller's team proved they are capable of putting Bo and his "three yards and a cloud of dust" philosophy behind them.

"They are the best football team we've ever played at Ole Miss, ever," said Mississippi Coach Billy Brewer. "They kept us spread out, and we didn't expect them to throw as much as they did." Neither, one could speculate, did millions of New Year's Day TV viewers!

Moeller's first real test will come, as he continues to replace graduating talent with kids he's recruited himself.

But it will be a long time before anyone comes along to replace Bo in the hearts of Michigan fans. Reminiscing about chastising a complaining player reveals much about how he felt about the long history and tradition of the Wolverines: "I leaned forward. My words were slow and deliberate. 'Now let me tell you something. . . . We brought you to the University of Michigan. The coaching staff here made you an All-Big-10 player. Your teammates elected you captain of the team. And you have the *audacity* to criticize Michigan football? How *dare* you?

"'I'd like to stand you up before all the guys who played here in the past, all those guys who won championships, went to bowl games, did all the things you want to do in college football, and I want you to tell them that your practices are too hard, that they're hitting too much, that you spend too much time watching film! And you know what they're going to tell you? Grow up! Grow up and be a man! And if you won't, then get the hell out of *Michigan football!*'"

Those Who Stay Will Be Champions, Bo's sign said. And he was right. Moeller will have success as well, because there is something about the Wolverines that transcends each coach, something even bigger than Bo. Winning tradition. Go Blue.

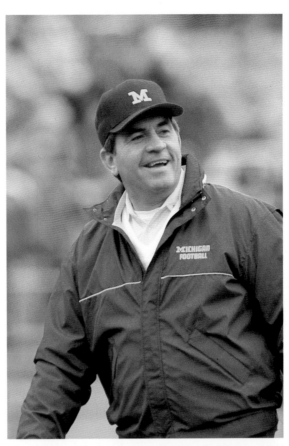

Left: *Long-time Assistant Coach Gary Moeller took over from Schembechler for the 1990 season, and led Michigan to a 9-3 record – including a Gator Bowl victory over Mississippi, 35-3.*

Below: *Go Blue: Another Wolverine team takes the field.*

Michigan Wolverines Football Record

YEAR-BY-YEAR RESULTS

Year	Coach	W	L	T	Pts	Opp
1879	None	1	0	1	1	0
1880	None	1	0	0	13	6
1881	None	0	3	0	4	28
1882	No Team					
1883	None	2	3	0	63	83
1884	None	2	0	0	36	19
1885	None	3	0	0	82	0
1886	None	2	0	0	74	0
1887	None	3	0	0	66	0
1888	None	4	1	0	130	40
1889	None	1	2	0	33	80
1890	None	4	1	0	129	36
1891	Mike Murphy & Frank Crawford	4	5	0	168	114
1892	Frank Barbour	7	5	0	298	172
1893	Frank Barbour	7	3	0	278	102
1894	William McCauley	9	1	1	244	84
1895	William McCauley	8	1	0	266	14
1896	William Ward	9	1	0	262	11
1897	Gustave Ferbert	6	1	1	166	46
1898	Gustave Ferbert	10	0	0	193	28
1899	Gustave Ferbert	8	2	0	176	43
1900	Langdon Lea	7	2	1	117	55
1901	Fielding Yost	11	0	0	550	0
1902	Fielding Yost	11	0	0	644	12
1903	Fielding Yost	11	0	1	565	6
1904	Fielding Yost	10	0	0	567	22
1905	Fielding Yost	12	1	0	495	2
1906	Fielding Yost	4	1	0	72	30
1907	Fielding Yost	5	1	0	107	6
1908	Fielding Yost	5	2	1	128	81
1909	Fielding Yost	6	1	0	116	34
1910	Fielding Yost	3	0	3	28	9
1911	Fielding Yost	5	1	2	90	38
1912	Fielding Yost	5	2	0	158	65
1913	Fielding Yost	6	1	0	175	21
1914	Fielding Yost	6	3	0	233	68
1915	Fielding Yost	4	3	1	130	81
1916	Fielding Yost	7	2	0	243	56
1917	Fielding Yost	8	2	0	304	53
1918	Fielding Yost	5	0	0	96	6
1919	Fielding Yost	3	4	0	93	102
1920	Fielding Yost	5	2	0	121	21
1921	Fielding Yost	5	1	1	187	21
1922	Fielding Yost	6	0	1	183	13
1923	Fielding Yost	8	0	0	150	12
1924	George Little	6	2	0	155	55
1925	Fielding Yost	7	1	0	227	3
1926	Fielding Yost	7	1	0	191	38
1927	Elton "Tad" Wieman	6	2	0	137	39
1928	Tad Wieman	3	4	1	36	62
1929	Harry Kipke	5	3	1	109	75
1930	Harry Kipke	8	0	1	111	23
1931	Harry Kipke	8	1	1	171	27
1932	Harry Kipke	8	0	0	123	13
1933	Harry Kipke	7	0	1	131	18
1934	Harry Kipke	1	7	0	71	143
1935	Harry Kipke	4	4	0	68	131
1936	Harry Kipke	1	7	0	36	127
1937	Harry Kipke	4	4	0	54	110
1938	Herbert "Fritz" Crisler	6	1	1	131	40
1939	Fritz Crisler	6	2	0	219	94
1940	Fritz Crisler	7	1	0	196	34
1941	Fritz Crisler	6	1	1	147	41
1942	Fritz Crisler	7	3	0	221	134
1943	Fritz Crisler	8	1	0	302	73
1944	Fritz Crisler	8	2	0	204	91
1945	Fritz Crisler	7	3	0	187	99
1946	Fritz Crisler	6	2	1	233	73
1947	Fritz Crisler	10	0	0	394	53
1948	Bennie Oosterbaan	9	0	0	252	44
1949	Bennie Oosterbaan	6	2	1	135	85
1950	Bennie Oosterbaan	6	3	1	150	114
1951	Bennie Oosterbaan	4	5	0	135	122
1952	Bennie Oosterbaan	5	4	0	207	134
1953	Bennie Oosterbaan	6	3	0	163	101
1954	Bennie Oosterbaan	6	3	0	139	87
1955	Bennie Oosterbaan	7	2	0	179	94
1956	Bennie Oosterbaan	7	2	0	233	123
1957	Bennie Oosterbaan	5	3	1	187	147
1958	Bennie Oosterbaan	2	6	1	132	211
1959	Chalmers "Bump" Elliott	4	5	0	122	161
1960	Bump Elliott	5	4	0	133	84
1961	Bump Elliott	6	3	0	212	163
1962	Bump Elliott	2	7	0	70	214
1963	Bump Elliott	3	4	2	131	127
1964	Bump Elliott	9	1	0	235	83
1965	Bump Elliott	4	6	0	185	161
1966	Bump Elliott	6	4	0	236	138
1967	Bump Elliott	4	6	0	144	179
1968	Bump Elliott	8	2	0	217	155
1969	Bo Schembechler	8	3	0	352	148
1970	Bo Schembechler	9	1	0	288	90
1971	Bo Schembechler	11	1	0	421	83
1972	Bo Schembechler	10	1	0	264	57
1973	Bo Schembechler	10	0	1	330	68
1974	Bo Schembechler	10	1	0	324	75
1975	Bo Schembechler	8	2	2	324	130
1976	Bo Schembechler	10	2	0	432	95
1977	Bo Schembechler	10	2	0	353	124
1978	Bo Schembechler	10	2	0	372	105
1979	Bo Schembechler	8	4	0	312	151
1980	Bo Schembechler	10	2	0	322	129
1981	Bo Schembechler	9	3	0	355	162
1982	Bo Schembechler	8	4	0	345	204
1983	Bo Schembechler	9	3	0	355	160
1984	Bo Schembechler	6	6	0	214	200
1985	Bo Schembechler	10	1	1	342	98
1986	Bo Schembechler	11	2	0	379	203
1987	Bo Schembechler	8	4	0	331	172
1988	Bo Schembechler	9	2	1	361	167
1989	Bo Schembechler	10	2	0	335	184
1990	Gary Moeller	9	3	0	389	198

BOWL RESULTS

The Bluebonnet Bowl – Houston, Texas
Record: 1-0
1981 – Michigan 33, UCLA 14

The Fiesta Bowl – Tempe, Arizona
Record: 1-0
1986 – Michigan 27, Nebraska 23

The Gator Bowl – Jacksonville, Florida
Record: 1-1
1979 – UNC 17, Michigan 15
1991 – Michigan 35, Mississippi 3

The Hall of Fame Bowl – Tampa, Florida
Record: 1-0
1988 – Michigan 28, Alabama 24

The Holiday Bowl – San Diego, California
Record: 0-1
1984 – BYU 24, Michigan 17

The Orange Bowl – Miami, Florida
Record: 0-1
1976 – Oklahoma 14, Michigan 6

The Rose Bowl – Pasadena, California
Record: 6-8
1902 – Michigan 49, Stanford 0
1948 – Michigan 49, USC 0
1951 – Michigan 14, California 6
1965 – Michigan 34, Oregon State 7
1970 – USC 10, Michigan 3
1972 – Stanford 13, Michigan 12
1977 – USC 14, Michigan 6
1978 – Washington 27, Michigan 20
1979 – USC 17, Michigan 10
1981 – Michigan 23, Washington 6
1983 – UCLA 24, Michigan 14
1987 – Arizona State 22, Michigan 15
1989 – Michigan 22, USC 14
1990 – USC 17, Michigan 17

The Sugar Bowl – New Orleans, Louisiana
Record: 0-1
1984 – Auburn 9, Michigan 7

Composite Bowl Record: 10-12

CAREER RUSHING RECORDS

Most Attempts	
Jamie Morris (1984-87)	809
Most Net Yards Rushing	
Jamie Morris (1984-87)	4393
Average Gain per Play	
Rob Lytle (1973-76)	5.96
Average Yards per Game	
Bill Taylor (1969-71)	102.4
Most Rushing Touchdowns	
Rick Leach (1975-78)	34

CAREER PASSING RECORDS

Most Attempted	
Steve Smith (1980-83)	648
Most Completed	
Jim Harbaugh (1983-86)	387
Most Yards Gained	
Jim Harbaugh (1983-86)	5449
Average Yards/Game	
Jim Harbaugh (1983-86)	175.8
Most TD Passes	
Rick Leach (1975-78)	48

CAREER RECEIVING RECORDS

Most Passes Caught	
Anthony Carter (1979-82)	161
Most Yards Gained	
Anthony Carter (1979-82)	3076
Average Yards/Reception	
Dick Rifenburg (1944-48)	24.1
Most TD Passes Caught	
Anthony Carter (1979-82)	37

CAREER SCORING RECORDS

Most Points Scored	
Mike Gillette (1985-88)	307
Most Touchdowns Scored	
Anthony Carter (1979-82)	40
Most Field Goals Scored	
Mike Gillette (1985-88)	57
Most PATs Scored	
Mike Gillette (1985-88)	130

ALL-AMERICANS

The following is a list of the University of Michigan's All-Americans by uniform number.

1 Paul Goebel	Butch Woolfolk	Ron Simpkins	63 Julius Franks	76 Stefan Humphries
Anthony Carter	25 Tom Edwards	41 Randy Logan	65 Reggie McKenzie	77 Arthur Walker
2 Jack Blott	Tom Curtis	Rob Lytle	Kurt Becker	Paul Seymour
3 Tripp Welborne	27 Benny Friedman	42 Billy Taylor	66 Mike Hammerstein	85 Lowell Perry
4 Jim Harbaugh	Charles Bernard	43 James Pace	67 Mervin Pregulman	86 Robert Westfall
6 Harry Kipke	28 Robert Timberlake	45 William Daley	John Vitale	John Anderson
Dave Brown	30 Harry Hawkins	Pete Elliott	69 Tom Dixon	87 Edward Frutig
7 Rick Leach	Brad Cochran	46 Harry Newman	70 Marty Huff	Ronald Kramer
11 Francis Wistert	32 E.R. Slaughter	47 Bennie Oosterbaan	71 Dave Gallagher	88 Elmer Madar
Albert Wistert	33 Mike Taylor	49 Robert Chappuis	72 Allen Wahl	Jim Mandich
Alvin Wistert	35 Tom Darden	Richard Volk	Dan Dierdorf	89 Richard Rifenburg
13 Garland Rivers	Don Dufek	50 Otto Pommerening	Walt Downing	95 Curtis Greer
17 Ted Petoskey	36 Ralph Heikkinen	57 Maynard Morrison	Ed Muransky	96 Calvin O'Neal
18 Chalmers Elliott	37 Jim Smith	59 George Lilja	John Elliott	98 Tom Harmon
19 Robert Brown	39 Henry Hill	60 Mark Donahue	75 William Yearby	
24 John Clancy	40 Ron Johnson	Mark Messner	William Paris	

In the early years of Michigan football, players did not wear numbers on their uniforms. Fourteen Wolverine All-Americans did not wear numbers:

William Cunningham	Germany Schulz	James Craig	John Maulbetsch	Frank Steketee
Neil Snow	Albert Benbrook	Miller Pontius	Cedric Smith	Henry Vick
William Heston	Stanfield Wells	Ernest Allmendinger	Frank Culver	

Index